Raising The Standard

BY

Wayne J. Edwards

A Pastor's Plea
For A
Return to Righteousness
In the Church

*"Awake to righteousness, and sin not;
for some have not the knowledge of God:
I speak this to your shame."*
(1 Corinthians 15:34)

xulon PRESS

Copyright © 2005 by Wayne J. Edwards

Raising The Standard
by Wayne J. Edwards

Printed in the United States of America

ISBN 1-59781-472-5

All rights reserved solely by the author. The author guarantees all contents are original and do not infringe upon the legal rights of any other person or work. No part of this publication may be reproduced, stored in a retrieval system or transmitted in any form by any means, electronic, mechanical, photocopy, recording or otherwise, without the prior permission of the author, except as provided by the USA copyright law. The views expressed in this book are not necessarily those of the publisher.

Unless otherwise indicated, Bible quotations are taken from the King James Version.

www.xulonpress.com

Dedicated to:

THE FAITHFUL
REMNANT
IN EVERY CHURCH
WHO FEEL LIKE THEY HAVE BEEN
RELEGATED
TO THE REAR OF THE SANCTUARY;
REMOVED
AS THOSE WHO NO LONGER MATTER!

Contents

Foreword *by Dr. Paul VanGorder* ix

Introduction xi

Chapter One:
The Lowering of the Standard – *The Loss of Reverence, Righteousness and Respect* 17

Chapter Two:
Raising the Standard – *In Our Love For God* 33

Chapter Three:
Raising the Standard – *In Our Love For Our Neighbor* 43

Chapter Four:
Raising the Standard – *In Our Love For The Church* 55

Chapter Five:
Raising the Standard – *In Our Worship Of God* 73
Part one: God's Desire For Our Worship 73
Part two: God's Design For Our Worship 94

Chapter Six:
Raising the Standard – *In Our Respect For The Word Of God* **115**

Chapter Seven:
Raising The Standard – *In Our Compassion For The Lost And In Our Preservation Of The Saved*............**135**

Chapter Eight:
Raising The Standard –
In Our Love For The Family **155**

Chapter Nine:
Raising The Standard – *Of The Lord Jesus Christ* **169**

Epilogue 179

Addendum: A Statement Added to the Baptist Faith and Message Regarding the Sanctity of Marriage and the Family 187

Statements of Sincere Appreciation 191

Foreword

In an age characterized by man's endeavors, human progress, and shallow proclamation of God's Word, how refreshing to hear and read solid exposition of the written Word. Such is the spoken ministry of God's servant, Wayne Edwards, now transposed to the printed page.

To borrow some words from C.H. Mackintosh:

"If ever there was a moment, in the history of the professing church, in which it behooved people to have divine authority for their path, and divine power to pursue it, this is that moment. There are so many conflicting opinions, so many jarring voices... that we are in danger of losing our balance."

With deep conviction grounded firmly in the inerrant Word and a commitment to live that Word, Edwards turns the searchlight of scripture upon the declining spiritual health in the church and its membership. No harping critic he. Like the Old Testament prophet, he deals with the sins of the saints. All the while, he makes clear the requirement for **"Raising the Standard!"**

> Dr. Paul VanGorder, writer for
> "Our Daily Bread" and Teacher for
> "The Day of Discovery," television
> ministry.

Introduction

In the wars of old, soldiers marched into battle by rank and file. For some, it would be their last moment of glory as they stood shoulder to shoulder with the men of their unit, bravely waiting the moment when they would face their enemy and fight to the death.

Just before the battle began, the command would be given for the standards to be raised. The first was the flag of their country, in whose name they had entered into war. The second was the flag of their division, a symbol identifying their particular unit or group, a rallying point for the soldiers to see and to return to when they became lost or confused in the midst of battle.

It was a disgrace for their standard to fall to the ground. So, if the assigned standard bearer became wounded and fell, another soldier would pick up that standard and carry it on, until he fell. And that process would continue until the last man had fallen. Historians tell us that, in the wars of old, the greatest number of bodies could be found near the standards. They died trying to hold them up.

According to the Bible, God has called the Church to be that standard of truth in a world of conflicting values; to be that moral conscience in a society that has an intrinsic bent toward evil. The Greek word for our English word "church" is *Ekklesia,* the called out and gathered ones. And, as that called-out community, Christians are to be the *"light of the world; (*that*) city on a hill* (that) cannot *be hidden."* (Matthew. 5:14 Emphasis mine) As followers of Jesus Christ, we are called to be *"a chosen race, a royal priesthood, a holy nation, a people for God's own choosing, that* (we) *may proclaim the excellencies of Him who has called* (us) *out of darkness into His marvelous light."* (1 Peter. 2:9 Emphasis mine) We are to *"prove* (ourselves*) to be blameless and innocent, children of God above reproach in the midst of a crooked and perverse generation, among whom* (we) *appear as lights in the world, holding fast the word of life."* (Philippians 2:15-16, Emphasis mine)

However, it is without question that the light of today's church has been dimmed. It has become weakened by a faulty (if not phony) connection to the power source of the Holy Spirit. In an effort to remove what appeared to be man-made barriers to the fellowship of the saints, the God-instituted standards for His church have been lowered. In what may have been a well-meaning effort to be all-inclusive; to reach out to those who are lost and unchurched, the church now welcomes and receives anyone and everyone into the family of God, without making sure of their confession of faith. The organized church may be larger than it has ever been before, if you look at the noses, nickels and noise. But I submit that the church today is weaker than ever before, and therefore that is why it is having little, if any, effect upon our world today.

The songwriter characterized Christians as soldiers in God's army, marching off to war, with the cross of Jesus, going on before. Since God called Abraham to follow Him, three watchwords have served as the standards for all of God's people to follow; **Reverence, Righteousness and Respect: Reverence,** meaning to love the Lord with all of our heart, soul, mind and strength, and to have no other gods before Him. **Righteousness,** meaning to love our neighbor as much as we love ourselves, as an example or illustration of how God loves us. **Respect,** meaning to live our lives in such a way that others would see our good works, and glorify our Father which is in heaven, as a witness to the world to the power of God to save us from our sin.

Today those three standards have fallen in dishonor and disgrace. In order to be acceptable to the world, many of today's church leaders have lowered these time-honored standards and replaced them with values that require less commitment and personal sacrifice on the part of their attenders. In the place of reverence, we now have **religion:** *"a form of godliness, although they have denied its power."* (2 Timothy 3:5) Righteousness has been replaced by personal **rights;** the freedom to live any way a person chooses, without restriction or restraint: *"lovers of self, lovers of money, boastful, arrogant, revilers, disobedient to parents, ungrateful, unholy, unloving, irreconcilable, malicious gossips, without self-control, brutal, haters of good, treacherous, reckless, conceited, lovers of pleasure rather than lovers of God."* (2 Timothy 3:2-4)

Finally, respect for the people of God has been replaced by **ruin** as the basic moral convictions of those within the Christian community are no different from those outside. Jesus said *"If the salt have lost his savor* (meaning its ability to preserve food from spoiling) *wherewith shall it be salted? It is thenceforth good for nothing, but to be cast out, and to be trodden under foot of men."* (Matthew 5:13)

Our Christian values are being trampled upon today because of the lack of personal integrity and moral virtue on the part of the majority of those who are raising the most fuss about the lack of moral values, and that includes a lot of preachers. During the past 40 years, laws have been passed restricting the expression of our basic Christian values, including the public display of Christian symbols, reading the Bible and praying in the schools or in the workplace, or even saying the pledge of allegiance. Since 1992, the government and the main-stream media elite have expressed such overt hostility toward Christians that not only are we no longer respected for our faith, we are being ridiculed because of our faith, primarily because they don't see us as being authentic.

Therefore, by not being different from the world, today's church is not making any difference in the world. As we look at the battles we, as believers, have fought over the last century, and especially those over the past 40 years, it saddens me to see that the Christian soldiers of our generation have let the standard of our Lord fall in dishonor. Like Lot's family, today's generation of Christians has become accustomed to the casual lifestyle of this evil world. As far as the culture in general, the contemporary Christian seems to enjoy the personal freedoms, the economic opportunities, the pleasures and the pastimes of our society just as much as the non-Christians do. As far as the Christian life in particular, the contemporary Christian seems to love the entertaining performances, the religious rituals and the less convicting tone of today's market-driven Christianity more than they the love the Lord, and therefore live by His Word. The truth is, by the lowering of our standards, we have allowed the banner of the cross to fall in dishonor. **But the greatest disgrace to our Lord is that there is no great cry among God's people that someone please raise that standard up again.**

The purpose of this book is well stated in 1 Corinthians 15:34 as the Apostle Paul exhorted his hearers to *"Awake to righteousness and sin not; for some have not the knowledge of God: I speak this to your shame."* It is also confirmed in his challenge to the Christians at Rome when he told them:

> *"It is high time to awake out of sleep; for now is our salvation nearer than when we believed. The night is*

far spent, the day is at hand; let us therefore cast off the works of darkness, and let us put on the armour of light. Let us walk honestly, as in the day; not rioting and drunkenness, not in chambering, and wantonness, not in strife and envying. But put ye on the Lord Jesus Christ, and make no provision for the flesh, to fulfill the lusts thereof." (Romans 13:11b-14)

This is one pastor's plea for a revival among God's people: a removal of worldly concepts and ideas about what it means to be a Christian, and a return to righteousness in the church. It is a critical analysis of the contemporary church movement and its negative impact upon the true purpose of the church, especially in regard to the work and witness of the church, our worship of God and our respect for His Word. It is a prophetic voice, sounding the alarm of what is ahead for the church, at least in America, unless God decides to send us a mighty, miraculous revival, and we return to Him.

With the exception of the first chapter, and a few revisions to the others, this material was first heard as sermons, by the dear folks at First Baptist Church, Forest Park, Georgia, as well as Westside Baptist Church, Titusville, Florida. Where possible, I have tried to give credit where credit is due regarding the information either cited or quoted. A list of resources has been included at the end of the book, not only as an outline of some of the materials read in the preparation of these sermons, but also as a suggestion for further reading in these more academic and intellectual sources, which are much more in depth in their particular subjects than I have attempted to be here. I am very grateful for their contribution to the furtherance of the gospel, which I pray is the end result of this labor of love.

CHAPTER ONE

The Lowering Of the Standards

The headline from the webpage of my own denomination said, *"Engage younger Christians...or else!"* Since I was in the middle of writing this book, the headline worked – it caused me to take the time to read the entire article. When I finished, I paused to thank the Lord for answered prayer, because I could not have asked for a better way to illustrate the burden of my heart for what is happening in the church today.

The article began with what the writer perceived as the crucial issue – *"a potential financial crisis looms for the Southern Baptist Convention as church members decrease denominational support."* Now, if the writer had stopped for a moment, perhaps called a few pastors of those churches where the denominational support had decreased, and had been willing to honestly face the consequences of what he would have heard, he may have been able to find the answer(s) as to why there has been a 30-year decline in giving by SBC church members. But instead he shifted to another report that said, *"millions of American 'twentysomethings' are checking out on organized Christianity.* And the rest of the article explained how today's young adults are less likely than any other age group to attend church, read the Bible or donate to religious causes, especially if they do not feel a personal connection to the ministry, and how the church had better change the way it relates to younger members and find some way to connect with them, because *"they won't buy into the same old, same old."*

Now here is my dilemma. Two groups of people are "checking out" on organized Christianity: those who are or have been involved in the church with their time, talents and tithes for years, and those who are not sure they want to get involved with traditional institutions, and even if they do get involved, they are less likely to support it with their time or talents, much less their tithe. And yet, at least to this pastor, it seems our whole concern today is for the second group rather than the first. In fact, those in the first group are being told in no uncertain terms to move over and make way for a new generation. And to offer any criticism at all to this activity is to question the will of God.

I believe many pastors have become so concerned about reaching the unchurched that they are **"unchurching" the churched!** In their zeal to do whatever it takes to attract a new generation of unbelievers to their church, whether saved or not, they are, at the same time, detracting the present and past generations of believers away from the church – those who helped buy the property, build the buildings, establish the organization, and who have faithfully supported the church for years. And sadly, statistics are showing, they are leaving the church by the droves; giving up, giving out, giving in – but they aren't "giving dollars" any more.

In her book, *Reaching Out Without Dumbing Down*, Marva J. Dawn cited a report given by David Barrett to Oxford Press, that *"in a twelve-month period, 2,765,100 worship attenders in Europe and North America cease to be practicing Christians – an average loss of 7,600 every day. This means that every week more than 53,000 people leave churches and never come back."* Dawn concludes, *"Something is seriously wrong if so many people do not find it worthwhile to continue participating in the Church!"* (*Reaching Out Without Dumbing Down: A Theology of Worship for This Urgent Time.* William B. Eerdmans Publishing Company, 1995). I could not agree more, **but it seems we are afraid to ask them why they are leaving!**

I have talked to some of these "de-churched" folks. These people have not given up on God or ceased to believe in Jesus Christ. These seasoned saints are being told that the tools God used to bring them to faith in Jesus Christ; methods that enhanced their love for God and encouraged them to grow in the grace and knowledge of the Lord; ministries that inspired them and motivated them to give, to go, to serve and to send; concepts that God has used to build His church for 2000 years are not relevant any more. Those who are writing the contemporary church growth manuals are saying the old disciplines of inductive Bible study, dynamic expository preaching, and the great hymns of our faith: world mission's conferences and such are actually barriers to unbelievers – hindrances that must be removed if we are to reach a new generation of lost people.

Pastors are being told by the church growth experts, if they want to attract unbelievers to their church, they must soften their preaching on sin, relax their convictions about the blood of Jesus Christ and change their music so that it sounds like the music of the world. They are being advised to use only paraphrased versions of the Bible, and to keep their "messages" short, because today's generation will not endure a lengthy lecture. They are being encouraged to insert current movie clips, interpretive dance, personal illustrations and other unique things, just to grasp their attention, and to spend the majority of their sermon time on personal application as opposed to biblical proclamation. One of the most ludicrous examples of this was a pastor who said he actually made his own recipe of salsa as a part of his "sermon" on how God wants every married couple to enjoy "hot sex!"

So, the church in America is being lulled to sleep with affluence, entertainment and a form of godliness, but without the true power of God. We have many great churches, if you look at the size of their buildings, their budgets and the baptisms they report. But the majority of churches today are nothing more than religious organizations, trying to attract the world with amateur theatre, synthesized music and engaging media. And the faithful remnant, those who sacrificed their time, talents and tithes to see the church begin, grow and develop are now being relegated to the rear of the sanctuary, or they are being systematically removed as those who no longer matter.

Why is there a lack of giving among today's church members toward denominational causes? Because the church has lost its vision of what Jesus has called it to do and to be. **The dumbing down of doctrine and theology has caused a weakening of our mission to get the whole Word to the whole world.** Therefore, not only are we not reaching the unchurched, because we have hidden the true gospel behind catchy phrases, acrostics and market-driven analysis so much that we no longer have any "good news" to tell them, but at the same time we have unchurched the churched, by abandoning the very methods God used in their lives to encourage their spiritual growth and maturity, which included our responsibility to fulfill the Great Commission, perhaps in our lifetime.

Today's Christians are content to defend their homes and families rather than to allow the Lord to use them in the world to make a difference. The majority of Christians today seem to be more interested in making sure they are getting all of the blessings God has promised them, rather than being a channel of God's blessings to the rest of the world. And in so doing, the church is missing some major opportunities to share the gospel in a world that has never been more ready to hear the truth than it is today. As Marva Dawn says in her book, *"While researchers are discovering that members of the boomer generation are searching for moral authority, multitudes of preachers are throwing theirs away."* (*Reaching Out Without Dumbing Down: A Theology of Worship for This Urgent Time,* William B. Eerdmans Publishing Company, 1995)

But according to the statistics, **the contemporary model of "church" isn't working either.** George Barna is the author of 35 books on American religious and cultural trends. He has conducted annual reviews of American religion since 2000 and has polled the country's religious temperature since 1984. In a recent article in the Washington Times, Barna noted the *"continued rise in the number of unchurched Americans."* He said the number of unchurched adults had *"nearly doubled from 38 million to 75 million in the past decade,"* the strongest trend, *"among men, people younger than 40, singles and people living in coastal states."* As far as the depth of American Christians' faith, Mr. Barna said, *"the typical American adult watches football games more often than he attends worship services."* (January 3-9, 2005 Washington Times)

In an article posted on The Church Report web page, Dr. Barna reported, *"Despite widespread efforts to increase church attendance across the nation, the annual survey of church attendance conducted by the Barna Group shows that one-third of all adults are unchurched. That proportion has changed little during the past five years. Of the nation's increasing population, the number of unchurched adults continues to grow by nearly a million people annually."* (May 17, 2005, Church Report Web Page, – A study of the Unchurched)

It seems that the same disinterest in church is occurring among the teenagers. Only 12% of today's teens attend a church of any denomination, according to published reports, and 80% of teenagers not only do not have a church home, they do not have a church history. It also seems the more churches adjust their worship styles to "attract" today's teens, the less they are impressed. With their ability to connect with each other via internet chat-rooms, "blogger" groups and text messaging, they just don't see the need for the fellowship of the church. For many young people, even from very solid, Christian homes, church is just another option for their involvement; a way to meet friends and have interaction, but not totally necessary for their spiritual needs.

It is reported that there were more than 3000 churches started in 2004. However, subtracting the churches that closed their doors, the net growth was less than 1%. Furthermore, the addition of new and different styles of churches did not increase church attendance. Even with the explosive growth of the megachurches, those with attendance of over 5000 per Sunday, overall church attendance is down 35% since 1970. (Cited in *A Better Way,* by Michael Horton, Baker Books, 2002)

I believe this low-standards, shallow-commitment, lackadaisical attitude among the "believers," those who "say" they believe in God, is the major contributing factor to the low moral standards we have in our society today. What onslaught of evil has the church been able to restrain over the past 35 years? What moral decadence have we been able to control or contain over the last generation? Other than inconsistent church attendance, what part of our moral base have we been able to preserve? Who would have thought we would be discussing such moral issues as we are today?

When I was in my twenties, the battle was over the abuse of alcohol, drugs and the negative influence of satanic music. In my thirties, the battle was to keep Bible reading and prayer in public schools and pornography out of the eyes of our children. When I reached fifty, concerned Christians were mounting an all-out war against divorce and the breakup of the family, abortion, homosexuality and the gay-day parade at Disney World.

But, which of those battles did we win? Not one of them! Either the "Moral Majority" wasn't as moral as was first thought, or it wasn't the majority after all. Either way, as Christians, **we lost the high ground, not because of our lack of motivation, but because of our own lack of spiritual integrity; we let our own standards down**. Because of our own lack of convictions, we have allowed our own nation to regress from what was, at least, a Christian-based society, to a post-Christian society and now to an anti-Christian society. As a result, we are now living in the very cesspool of sin. The abuse of drugs and alcohol continues to infect our lives, lewd and vulgar mantras have become today's style of music, pornography and promiscuity are flaunted in everything from entertainment to clothing styles for little children, one out of every two marriages, even among believers, end in divorce, and the church is impotent to even take a stand against these moral issues.

Today, many battles are being fought within the Christian community. Some Christians are trying to preserve the sanctity of marriage as being that sacred union between a man and a woman. Others, who also call themselves Christians, see nothing wrong with a homosexual marriage or the ordination of homosexual priests. Some Christians are crying out against those who want to use stem cells from aborted babies as a potential cure for some of our horrible diseases. Others shake their heads at such narrow-minded naivety and see nothing wrong with even growing a fetus in a Petri dish just to harvest whatever cells they need to extend their own life. To one group it is an issue of the truth of God's Word. To another it is an issue of God's love. But the real issue is that the unbelieving world is looking on and wondering about our God.

Our nation is at war with a fanatical element of the fastest growing religion in the world, Islam. And while some who have embraced this false religion as their way to heaven, are, in their heart of hearts, people of peace, it is without question that the basic tenet of Islam is the elimination of the "infidels" – those who do not believe in the god of Allah, and who will not convert to their way of life And while this war is being fought on a military battlefield with bullets and bombs, at its core is a religious war between those who believe in the god of the Koran and those who believe in the God of the Bible.

But, in the name of tolerance, **many of today's Christian leaders have acquiesced and said that Jesus is not the only way to the Father**; that all faiths are the same as long as one truly believes. Others have avoided the subject all together for fear of being attacked or ridiculed as being judgmental. In so doing, we are allowing our children to believe in a plurality of gods; that all are equal. For sure, we live in a pluralistic society that is based upon an anti-Christian philosophy of life. But, if we are to continue to raise up a godly heritage of our Christian faith, we had better raise the standard of reverence, meaning there is but *"one God, one faith, one Lord, one hope, one baptism"* (Ephesians 4:5), and only one way to true salvation, and that is through our faith in the person and the work of Jesus Christ upon the cross.

In 2004, our generation witnessed one of the most devastating disasters ever to be recorded in human history, the Tsunami in Asia. Over 200,000 people were swept into eternity without warning, the majority of them having placed their faith in the false religions of Hinduism and Buddhism. When the unbelieving world asked why God allowed this to happen, rather than acknowledging the power and authority of our sovereign God to do as He wills, and man's need to always be prepared to face eternity by placing his faith in the person of Jesus Christ, some of our most respected Christian leaders were at a loss for words. Instead of witnessing to the saving grace of God through Christ, they wimped-out in unbelief, not willing to even mention the greater judgment of God which is to come upon those who do not believe in Jesus.

As far as the war in Iraq and the other skirmishes around the world, we may be able to write a contract of peace; an agreement to the temporary cessation of military conflict, but it will only be for a season. According to the Bible there will not be true peace until the Prince of Peace comes to rule and to reign upon the earth. We can pray for peace and work for peace, and we should. But let us also remember that it is during these times of chaos and conflict that we can point out to those who are lost that this world has never known, nor will it ever know, true peace until the Lord Jesus comes. But we can also witness to them about the peace that passes understanding that God gives to those who put their faith and trust in Jesus Christ.

At the beginning of the war in Iraq, many churches held specific prayer meetings for our soldiers and their families, our nation's leaders and their families, and for those whom we must now refer to as our enemies. But as the days, weeks and months have progressed, we have become accustomed to the body count, jaded by the news of even more suicide bombers, emboldened by the recent elections and hopeful as we sense that the end may be in sight. The fact is there may be many more days of fighting and many more people may die. I believe the church needs to seize this opportunity, not only to send missionaries to assist our soldiers in their quest for freedom, but to challenge to our own spiritual growth; to help us see this world through the eyes of Christ, and to respond as He gives us direction.

We can also be encouraged by the outpouring of love

and support that has been given to the survivors of the tsunami. Within hours, Christian organizations were on the ground offering food, medicine, clothing and comfort to those who had lost loved ones. Some churches organized groups of people to serve as a rotating army of helpers to the relief agencies who will be there for the duration, and we need to be in prayer for them, for not since Nagasaki and Hiroshima have we seen such devastation.

But again, while we can be thankful for those who have given, and those who have gone, I believe we will one day stand ashamed in the presence of our Lord for what we did compared to what we should be doing even now. This door of opportunity for us to share the love of Jesus will soon be closed, as the governments of those nations become suspect of our motives and intentions. In a few years the physical and financial impact upon that part of the world will be nothing but a memory; an entry on the record books of those who catalogue the "catastrophic acts of God" upon the earth. But will it also be remembered as a time when the world stood in awe at the gigantic outpouring of the love of God's people for those in need? Will they remember our good works and glorify our God which is in heaven? Will they have a greater respect for the Church of the Lord Jesus Christ?

From the classroom to the courtroom, from the schoolhouse to the White House, from our neighborhoods to the nations, **God is opening up one opportunity after the other for us to show the world who we are and who our God is.** God has even created a crisis where Christians might manifest the mighty power of God's love. (See Amos 4-5) But the church has become so blinded by its own self interests and caught up in its own convenient causes that it has lost sight of its true purpose in the world.

Truly, the harvest is ripe and ready, but the laborers are few. Why? As stated before, **the majority of God's people live with no sense of responsibility toward those who are**

lost. They see nothing wrong with hoarding the resources God has blessed them with, while there are millions of people, whom God has created in His own image, and for His glory, who have never heard of the name of Jesus Christ. But God has given us that responsibility, not for their salvation, but to be His witnesses. The day of accountability will be soon!

God created us to worship Him – to glorify Him and to praise His Holy Name forever! However, rather than created man worshiping His Creator God, as God designed and desires, man has re-created "god" in his on image, and he is worshiping that image of god, rather than God Himself. By lowering his concept of God, man also lowered the biblical standards of godliness; what it means to be holy, righteous and acceptable unto God. And in so doing, he lowered the unbelieving world's concept of God, their need for Him, and even His power to deliver them from sin.

The irrefutable evidence that we are drawing closer to the Lord in our worship, our walk and our witness is that we are able to see this world for what it really is, and not what we would like to believe it is. Then we will be willing to go where we are sent, and do what we are sent to do, in order to make a difference. Since we are not seeing that happen in and through the church today, **the only conclusion one can draw is that the glory of God has departed from the majority of churches**. The sad thing is many of the church members are so caught up in maintaining the ministry machinery they do not realize the Holy Spirit is missing.

The reason there is so much confusion about what a church ought to do and to be today is because **we have forgotten what it means to be the Body of Christ in the world today.** Some believers are trying to make the church fit their own concept of what they think the church ought to do and be. It's exactly what the Christian Philosopher Francis Schaffer said in the 1970's would be happening in the church in the 1990's. He called it *"radical individualism,"* where everyone worships their own concept of God rather than the God of the Bible who has been revealed to us through Jesus Christ. The great puritan writer, J.I. Packer referred to it as *"hot tub religion,"* the philosophy that Jesus is there to answer their prayers and the church is there to meet their needs – no concern about true doctrine, theology or the other essential issues of THE faith; no concern about missions or about witnessing or whether their worship is acceptable unto God; their only concern is *how the church can meet their needs!*

But this carnal concept of the church didn't begin in our generation. In fact, the church has always struggled with this to some degree. It was happening in the church at Corinth, which is why the Apostle Paul was so stern in his first letter to them regarding what he called their carnal behavior – dividing up into little groups because of their personal preferences and opinions – arguing over who was the best preacher or pastor – the very same things we hear today. Paul said this kind of behavior not only revealed their lack of spiritual growth, but, because they were *"walking like mere men"* (1 Corinthians 3:4), as far as their witness for Christ, they were no different from those who were unsaved.

But it was during the Great Awakenings of the 18th century, when a major shift occurred in the doctrine of the church, the results of which are still affecting the church today. The 18th century was the era of the great revivals where the Holy Spirit moved upon the church in ways the people had not seen before, and thousands of people were gloriously saved in revival crusades all across Europe and then to America. But rather than give God the glory for the great things He had done, man began to see how he could produce those same results through different methods and techniques, in the hopes of keeping the revival going.

Man's passion for God and passion for truth was

replaced by a passion for lost souls, and the theology of pragmatism began to take hold. Whatever brought more "souls" to Christ or attracted more people to the church had to be right because it was "working!" It appeared that God was blessing the method or that God had anointed the man. The purpose of the Sunday worship services shifted from being focused upon God and how His people could honor Him, to the needs of lost people and how the church could reach out to them. And the spotlight of glory shifted from Jesus Christ, the Savior of all men, to those men who could attract the most people by their charismatic personality or their particular methods or style of preaching or singing. Over the years, many churches, and even many denominations tried to copy those methods in order to take advantage of, or perhaps even profit from, what appeared to be a great harvest of souls and a great revival of the church.

But whenever there is such a paradigm shift in any organization, there is a gain/loss ratio that must be reviewed. **For every gain that was made by some manipulative method to reach the lost, there was a loss of doctrinal and theological truth**, as basic convictions were compromised by the very method itself. For every gain in converts by the schemes of men there was a lack of spiritual understanding on the part of the new believer, and that lack of discipleship resulted in a lack of spiritual growth, and therefore the loss of true, biblical worship. **What was gained by the numbers in attendance and in converts in all of these extremes was negated by the loss of biblical certainty and theological integrity**. But more importantly, the glory that rightfully belonged to Jesus Christ, and Jesus Christ alone, was diverted to man.

It wasn't long until new groups were being formed about certain beliefs, such as the Pentecostal movement in the early 1900's and the Charismatic movement of the 1950's and 1960's, where the various manifestations of the

Holy Spirit became equal to, if not more important than, the absolute truth of the Word of God. By the 1990's, people were driving to Pensacola, Florida, or Toronto, Canada, to get in on what they perceived to be the blessings of God.

Today, we are seeing the perpetual innovation of the church as it adapts to the changing needs of people, and as it adopts the changing philosophies of the church, without ever questioning whether or not they are acceptable unto God. Today, churches are using every gimmick imaginable to attract people to their "brand" of Christianity. Trite and trivial logos have replaced the true Logos. Terms such as "user-friendly" and "seeker-sensitive" have replaced "Christ exalting and God honoring!" The worship services are orchestrated to bypass the mind and to excite the emotions, so that everyone leaves feeling good about themselves, even though they have not learned one thing about the sovereignty of God or about His absolute authority over our lives

In Ephesians 3:1-21, the Apostle Paul outlined God's eternal plan and purpose for the church. **Paul makes it clear that the purpose of the church is not to bring glory to a man, nor to the works of a man, but to the One who began the church by the shedding of His own precious blood**, and the One who holds the church together today by His love, even Jesus Christ, our Lord. Because of that, to some degree the honor of the Lord Jesus Christ is in the hands of the church today. And because of that, what is done in every church on the Lord's Day will either bring glory to the Lord or glory to man. If it is done in the power of the flesh, no matter how well intended, it will *fall short of the glory of God* and will only serve to glorify man. But if it is done in the power of the Holy Spirit, and it lifts up the name of Jesus Christ as Lord, it will not only draw men to receive Jesus Christ as their Savior and Lord, but it will glorify God throughout all ages, world without end.

We have seen, and are seeing today, what happens in and

through the church when the standards are lowered. It is time for the standards to be raised again. It is time the church began to follow the model of the true, New Testament church, as outlined in Acts 2:41-47. The people were in harmony with each other, in agreement over the purpose of their fellowship, involved in the pursuit of truth through the teaching of the Apostles doctrine, praising God in their times of worship at the temple and in their homes, in prayer of thanksgiving for what God was doing, in favor with believers and unbelievers alike, *"And the Lord was adding to their number day by day those who were being saved."*

CHAPTER TWO

The Raising Of the Standard In Our Love For God

Jesus Christ left His Church in the world to be a standard bearer of His righteousness. He said, as His followers, Christians are to be as lights, shining brightly against the darkness of the sin and depravity of our society. He said Christians are to act as salt, preserving our society from total decay. But the most recent surveys show the behavior of many church members today is not any different from that of unbelievers. In things like dress codes, physical appearance, choice of entertainment, how we make a living, or how we spend our money – even our attitudes toward sexual behavior, marriage and divorce, our moral conduct is not that much different than those who have never professed to know Jesus Christ as their Savior and Lord.

Not only have we compromised our convictions in order to not offend the unholy world, but we are participating in things that are an offense to a Holy God. Behavior God specifically condemned in the life of His chosen people is no longer considered "sin" by the majority of God's people today. Think about each one of the Ten Commandments and you will find areas where, as a church body, we have let those standards down. Did God say they were commandments to be obeyed or suggestions to be considered?

A lot of Christians raised their voices when the Supreme Court ruled that the carved image of the Ten Commandments had to be removed from the courthouse in Alabama. In protest, millions of Christians began to display a plastic sign of the Ten Commandments in their yard or in the windows of their business. Perhaps they have forgotten that those two stone tablets were broken into smithereens when Moses came down from the mountain and found God's people "playing" at worship. Perhaps they have forgotten that those God-ordained laws are now inscribed upon our hearts. Perhaps they are more concerned about them being displayed than obeyed! Perhaps they are more concerned about the actions of the Supreme Court than the soon coming judgment of the Supreme Lord.

But where do we begin in restoring our moral standards? Rather than looking at where we have failed or how we have let those standards down, I believe we need to see Who we have failed and Who we have let down, and His name is Jesus.

In His message to the church at Ephesus, Jesus said *"I have somewhat against thee, because thou hast left thy first love."* (Rev. 2:4) Notice that Jesus didn't say the church had *lost* their first love, but that they had *left* it! They had allowed many other things, perhaps even some good things, to get in the way of the best thing, which is to love the Lord Jesus.

Could that be said of the church today? Have we left our first love? Do we love our religious organizations and activities, even our own church family, more than we love the Lord? Could that be said of each one of us today? Have we left our first love for the Lord? Do we have that same love for God we had on that first day when we discovered He truly loved us?

I believe the first place we must begin in raising the

standard of our Lord is in our love for God. We must remove anything from our heart except our pure devotion to the Lord Jesus Christ. Jesus said it this way in Matthew 22:34-40: *"Thou shalt love the Lord thy God with all thy heart, and with all thy soul, and with all thy mind."* In essence, we are to love God with our whole heart, not just the little piece of it we offer to Him each Sunday.

The word "heart" here refers to our devotion. Whatever we attach our affections to we become devoted to, whether they are good or bad things. Therefore Jesus said we are to become "attached to" or "totally devoted" to God, not to things about God, such as symbols, music, concepts, ideas or philosophies about Him. As Jesus said in Matthew 6:21, *"For where your treasure is,* (meaning the object of your affection) *there will your heart* (or your devotion) *be also."* (Emphasis mine) And our devotion belongs only to God.

You remember the account of the rich, young ruler who asked Jesus what he could do to inherit eternal life. He said that he had kept the commandments of God, even from the days of his childhood, but that he still lacked something in his heart. Jesus told him to go and sell all he had and give the money to the poor, and then he could have treasure in heaven, and he could be a follower of Christ.

But the Bible says that young man walked away sorrowful, because he was very rich and didn't want to give up his possessions. He had a divided heart, which Jesus knew about, and was trying to get the young man to see. But this young man loved his riches more than he loved the Lord, or more than he desired to have eternal life. In other words, the object of his affections (his riches) determined the direction of his devotion.

Christians today have divided hearts, which is why most of them are very sorrowful. Like the rich young ruler, they may have many things to make them externally happy, but they are, at the same time, intrinsically unhappy because their wealth cannot buy them contentment with God. What happened to cause this dichotomy of the heart?

On the day they received Jesus Christ as their Savior and surrendered unto Him as their Lord, whether they fully understood it or not, conceptually, if they were seriously saved, they surrendered their heart unto the Lord and gave Him absolute authority over their lives. But, as life moved on, their affections changed, and so did their devotion. They met someone they wanted to marry, and they said they loved them with all of their heart. They found a work they liked to do, and a place in which to do it, and they said they put their whole heart into it. They found some land and built their house, and they loved that dream home with all of their heart. As the children came along, they said they loved them will all of their heart. The list could go on and on, with each new thing drawing their affections away from their initial desire to love God with their whole heart, and re-directing their devotions to the things of the world, or even the things of God, or about God, rather than to God Himself. They have a divided heart, which means they are divided in their desires and in their duties. They are neither hot nor cold toward God. They are lukewarm, indifferent, because they "left" that first love.

And then, just as it did with the rich young ruler, conviction comes upon them in the form of dissatisfaction or discontentment. They have all these things, but there is still something lacking in their heart; something is missing. They know it is the Lord, but they can't give up their riches, their temporal possessions, pursuits and pleasures to reconnect with the One they once said they loved with all of their heart. And in so doing, they begin to compromise their convictions, lower the standards of righteousness in their walk with the Lord, rationalize and justify their decision by saying, *"Everybody is doing it!"* And then, they just learn to live with that divided heart. There is no joy in the Lord, and therefore no strength to live the Christian life. There is no righteousness in their walk with the Lord, and therefore no witness to the world. Religious activity is just a weekly salve to try to soothe the pain of their hurting heart.

Where are the affections of your heart right now? The Apostle John exhorted us to:

> *"Love not the world, neither the things that are in the world. If any man love the world, the love of the Father is NOT in him. For ALL THAT IS IN THE WORLD, the lust of the flesh, and the lust of the eyes and the pride of life, is not of the Father, but is of the world. And the world passeth away, and the lust thereof; but he that doeth the will of God abideth forever."* (1 John 2:15-17, Emphasis mine)

I love my wife of almost 40 years. She is my sweetheart and my dearest friend. I love our son, and his dear wife, and our precious granddaughter. They bring joy to my heart like no other persons on earth can do. I love my other relatives; they have a special place in my life. I love a small community of people near Managua, Nicaragua, they have become like family to us, and we think about them and pray for them regularly. I love God's creation and enjoy the beauty and splendor of it. I take pride in where I live and how I live and try my best to take care of the things God has blessed me with and entrusted to my care. The passion of my heart is to preach God's Word and to see Christians grow in the grace and knowledge of God, and I pour my heart into that every week.

God gave us the capacity to care for all people, and the desire to love some people very deeply. But the fact is everything in this world is going to pass away one day; it will soon be ashes. Every human relationship is temporary, at least on this side of heaven. The work we do down here will be nothing but wood, hay and stubble, unless our efforts bring glory to the Lord and can be used for the advancement of His kingdom, and not our own. The only thing that gives purpose and meaning and value to all of those other things is God Himself, and therefore He deserves our devotion. We are to love Him with our whole heart, and then allow His love to flow through us into the "things" of this world, including our human relationships.

But not only did Jesus say we are to love God with our whole heart, but we are to also love God with our whole soul. When God breathed into the lifeless body of Adam, he became a living soul. There may be some room for debate here, but I am convinced that the soul is divided into three parts: our mind – which gives us the capacity to think; our emotions – which give us the capacity to feel; and our will – which gives us the capacity to decide. The very breath of God separated man from the rest of creation, in that man was given a free will, even the ability to reject the gift of God's love.

The evidence that we truly love God with our whole soul is that our minds are concentrating upon God, our emotions are centered upon God and our will is surrendered unto God. 1 John 2:5 says *"But whoever KEEPS HIS WORD, in him the love of God has truly been perfected. BY THIS we know that we are in Him."* (NASB Emphasis mine) So, if someone says they love God with their whole soul, it means they are living in total obedience to God's will and God's ways.

Jesus said if we loved Him we would obey His commandments. *"Why do you call me, Lord, Lord, and do not the things which I say?"* (Luke 6:46) Again, the evidence of our love for God is our obedience to God, and to His word, and our willingness to make whatever sacrifice required to prove that love unto Him. Let me give you some examples.

A child may say he loves his parents with all of his heart, and he should. But when that child is requested to do something that is against his will, the child will evidence his real love for his parents by his obedience to them, even when it goes against what he thinks or even how he feels. A child also needs to love his parents with his whole soul, which means he will obey them.

Parents may say they love their children with their whole heart, and they should. But that love must be more than emotion or else the child will have nothing to eat or to wear and it will not live very long. So, parental love must also include a commitment to provide for and take care of their children. That's the love of the soul.

A husband and wife say they love each other with their whole heart, and they should, if they plan to stay married very long. But that love must be more than physical attraction or friendly affection if it is to be a "forever" love. That commitment will require a daily, uncompromising separation of themselves to each other. It will require a daily, unlimited dedication of themselves to each other. And sooner or later one of them will be required to surrender; yea, even die to himself/herself, in order to save that marriage. The strength of their love will be made evident by the willingness of the one to love the other, even with the other is not deserving of that love. The true love of the heart is made evident through the love of the soul, the love of obedience.

So, when Jesus said we are to love God with our whole soul, He is saying that we are to fully surrender our will unto His will, and be willing to make whatever sacrifice may be required to prove our love unto Him. And when that is being done, the love of God is being perfected in us.

There are many Christians today who say they love God with their whole heart. *"They sing and pray both night and day; hands raised in the air, praising God for His care. But when He asks them for a sacrifice, they say, "Well, that might be nice!" And they turn and look the other way, and just continue to sing and pray!"*

I believe the main reason the standard of our Lord is being dishonored today is because many Christians have never surrendered unto Jesus Christ as Lord, and therefore do not know how to live in total obedience to His word. They aren't willing to pay the price of separation from the world, which may include persecution, ridicule, scorn, rejection and often condemnation. They aren't willing to make the sacrifices necessary to "perfect" their love for God, which may include saying "no" to some things others say "yes" to, and saying "yes" to some things others say "no" to. Such a decision might also include some severe testing, whether physically, emotionally or spiritually; tests even designed and allowed by the Lord to determine the depth of our devotion to Him. Such a decision would also include our willingness to obey Him, even when we don't understand what He is doing or why. Only then will we know what it means to love God with our whole soul.

Jesus said we are to love the Lord with our whole heart, our whole soul. But He also said we are to love Him with our whole mind. God gave us a mind to think with, to reason with, to comprehend with and to decipher what is truth and what is false, and what should be kept in our memory and what should be cast aside.

The Apostle Paul said we should be *"Casting down imaginations, and every high thing that exalteth itself against the knowledge of God, and bringing into captivity every thought to the obedience of Christ." (2 Corinthians 10:5)* Does that mean we are never to read a non-Christian book or a newspaper or watch a television program? No! But what it does mean is that we will have formed a base of God's truth in our minds, through which every thought can be sifted to see if it is to be believed as received, or cast aside, because it is contrary to what we already know to be the truth of God's Word.

King David said he had hidden God's Word in his heart

so he would not sin against God. He had so memorized the laws and precepts of God's Word that he was wise to the ways of the world, and of the wicked, and he could avoid their snare.

In Romans 12:2, the Apostle Paul exhorted his readers to *"Be not conformed to this world; but be ye transformed by the RENEWING OF YOUR MIND, that ye may prove what is that good, and acceptable and perfect will of God."* (Emphasis mine) In Philippians 4:8, Paul wrote *"Whatsoever things are true, whatsoever things are honest, whatsoever things are just, whatsoever things are pure, whatsoever things are lovely, whatsoever things are of good report; if there be any virtue and if there be any praise, THINK on these things."* (Emphasis mine)

Oh, my friend, we are to THINK about the cross, and never forget the price Jesus paid for our salvation. We are to THINK about that empty tomb, and be reminded of our victory over sin, death and the grave. We are to THINK about what Jesus told us to do on this earth while He is now in heaven. We are to THINK about His promise to come again and take us out of this world and to live with Him forever. And the joy of that thought alone should fill our hearts so full of expectant joy that the unbelieving world would want to know the reason for our hope.

We cannot blame our moral failures and our lack of convictions upon the world or the influence of others. If we fall for Satan's lie today, it will not be because someone talked us into it, or the influence of the world caused us to compromise our convictions. It will be because, at that moment, we ceased to love the Lord our God with our whole heart, our whole soul, and our whole mind – we ceased to be obedient unto God.

The first standard that must be raised by the Church is our love for the One who saved us. We must move beyond the extrinsic love of our emotions to that intrinsic love of our heart, our soul and our mind. For the only motivation powerful enough to move us to a higher standard of righteous living in an unrighteous world, is our love for the Lord, thy God.

We may bow our heads in reverence or serve Him out of fear! But when we THINK of all He's done for us, how can we not love Someone so dear....as Jesus?

CHAPTER THREE

The Raising Of the Standard In Our Love For Our Neighbors

Until our Lord returns, the Church is to serve as His body in the world. As believers we are to be the standard-bearers to the rest of the world. By our lives, we are to be God's models of righteousness and holiness before the world. In our actions and attitudes, we are to exhibit God's standards of purity, decency, honesty and integrity. As we have said before, we are to be the salt and light in a sin-decaying and sin-darkening world.

But when we see those standards being lowered by an unbeliever, or even by a fellow believer, our mission is not to point fingers, or criticize, condemn or even complain. Our mission is to pray for those who have fallen, and **to raise that very standard even higher in our own lives,** so that our fellow soldiers will continue to fight on to victory, and so the unbelieving world will know that we will not quit until we have claimed the victory which is already ours in Christ Jesus.

If we are going to raise the standard in our own lives, we must be sure that we are not only indwelt by the Holy Spirit, which means we have been born again, but that we are also filled and empowered by the Holy Spirit to fight against the devil. The Apostle Paul made this clear in Ephesians 6:11-18 when he said the believer must daily *"Put on the whole armor of God, that (he) may be able to stand against the wiles of the devil. For we wrestle not against flesh and blood, but against principalities, against powers, against rulers of the darkness of this world, against spiritual wickedness in high places."*

Our battle is not with individuals, but with the devil himself. We don't raise the standard of Jesus Christ with words and actions of hatred against those who disagree with us. Yes, there are people whose voices and pens are being used to attempt to tear down every scriptural and traditional value we hold dear. And yes, their agenda is very clear. Their goal is to redefine truth to fit in with their sinful lifestyle, and they are being very successful in their pursuit of every form of earthly pleasure.

But physical violence and name calling, marching up and down the street with caustic signs, or even demanding our rights as equal citizens is not the way our Lord taught us to fight against our enemies. We are not to fight in the flesh, but in the Spirit. We are not to fight with our fists, but on our knees. We are not to fight with our opinions, but with the Word of truth, spoken in love.

In Matthew 22:34-40, Jesus took the Ten Commandments and comprised them into two statements of equal value. **He said the greatest commandment of all is to love God with our whole heart, our whole soul and our whole mind. Then He said,** *"Thou shalt love thy neighbor as thyself."* Jesus said, the outward manifestation of our love for God will be made known by our love for our fellow man, whether Christian or not.

The first time the Bible records this commandment about loving thy neighbor is in Leviticus 19:18 where Moses wrote *"Thou shalt not avenge, nor bear any grudge against the children of thy people, but thou shalt love thy neighbor as thyself: I am the Lord."* And, if you read chapters 15-19 of Leviticus, you can see all the specific examples Moses gave to illustrate or demonstrate that one single command.

Luke records that Jesus referred to it again when a lawyer asked Him what he could do to inherit eternal life. Jesus asked him what was written in the law, and the man quoted these two commandments from Leviticus. Jesus said: *"Thou hast answered right: do this and thou shalt live."* *(Luke 10:27)* The implication of the context is that our obedience to these commands reveals a heart that is prepared for heaven!

But it was the Apostle Paul who exposed the real meaning of this commandment in his letter to the Romans when he wrote: *"Owe no man anything but to love one another; for he that loveth another hath fulfilled the law. For this, though shalt not commit adultery, thou shalt not kill, thou shalt not bear false witness, thou shalt not covet; and if there be any other commandment, it is briefly comprehended in this saying: THOU SHALT LOVE THY NEIGHBOR AS THYSELF. Love worketh no ill to his neighbor; therefore love is the fulfilling of the law."* (Romans 13:8-10, Emphasis mine)

It is amazing to think that the one law that embraces all others is our love for others. Our love for each other as believers, and even our love for unbelievers will do more to draw men and women to Jesus Christ than anything else we could ever do. Jesus even said our love for each other in the Body of Christ would convince the unbelieving world that we are Christians. (John 10:35)

If there is one area in our walk with the Lord where we need to raise the standard, it is in our love for each other, and for others. Our profession to love God with our whole heart, soul and mind must be manifested by our demonstration of genuine love for others. Otherwise, our profession is mere hypocrisy! What we do in church every Sunday, the singing of hymns, the reading of the scriptures, even the preaching of the Word and prayer; none of it will make any difference, even in our own lives, if it is not reflected in how we love others, even those outside the church. We are to love our neighbors as much as we love ourselves, meaning, as Christians, we are to love non-Christians as much as we love each other! (This theme will be further developed in another chapter)

The phrase *"thou shalt"* makes this more than a good idea or a helpful suggestion. This is, first of all, a command to be obeyed. The word "command" is a military term that is used to call the troops to action. It is an issue of orders to be followed. It is a regulation to be honored. Our Commanding Officer, the Lord Jesus, has called us to attention and to action. And the command He has given to us is to love our neighbors the same way He loves us.

In John 13:34-35, Jesus told His disciples *"A new commandment I give unto you, that ye love one another; as I have loved you, that ye also love one another. By this shall all men know that ye are my disciples, if ye HAVE love one to another."* (Emphasis mine)

It is obvious from these words from the lips of our loving Lord that the weapon of our war against the sin in this world is the same as His weapon against the sin in our heart. *"For God so loved!"* (John 3:16) The weapon of our warfare is love, and we have been given the command to go into the world and use it against our enemies.

The problem is, we don't see this as a command to be obeyed, but rather an idea to be debated. We have neighbors all around us and God has given to us the most effective weapon in the world to win their hearts to Him, which is love. And He has given us our marching orders to go into the world and use that weapon of love against our enemies. But many of our soldiers are still standing in formation, waiting for someone to lead the way. Or, they have retreated to the safe zones, away from the conflicts at the battlefront. Others have absolutely gone AWOL to fulfill their selfish desires of life, or they have just surrendered to the enemy and are being held captive to his lies.

If a military soldier did this, he would find himself in the stockade, branded as being a coward at best and a traitor at worst, because he disobeyed orders and abandoned his duty in the midst of the battle. **And it is no wonder that the world is so full of hatred and bitterness today, because the majority of the church is absent without leave and living in disobedience to our Lord's command.** We have allowed His standard of love to fall into the pits of sin. And again, I repeat this statement. Perhaps the greatest sin of all is that there is no great cry, no outrage, even among the majority of Christian leaders that the standards of our faith have fallen into disrepute.

But not only did Jesus give us a command to be obeyed, but He also gave us a commission to be accepted: *"Thou shalt LOVE THY NEIGHBOR!"* Immediately, we are faced with two questions: What does He mean by love? What does He mean by neighbor?

The first question is easily answered by looking at two very familiar passages of scripture. The first is John 3:16, perhaps the most memorized verse in the entire Bible. Read it again, slowly and carefully: *"For God SO LOVED the world that HE GAVE His only begotten Son!"* (Emphasis mine) Did you get it? God LOVED, God GAVE! The next passage is Romans 5:8: *"God COMMENDETH His love toward us, in that while we were yet sinners, Christ died for us."* (Emphasis mine) God demonstrated His love toward us, in that while we were still sinning against Him, He allowed His only begotten Son to die for us! This is the kind of love the Father has for the kind of folks like us!

So, what does Jesus mean when He said we are to

LOVE our NEIGHBOR? It means we are to sacrifice ourselves, if necessary, to communicate our genuine love for them and to them, just as God did for us. It means we are to look beyond their faults and find the need in their lives, and be prepared to do whatever it takes to fill that need with the love that was shed abroad in our hearts the very instant we were born again. To love our neighbor is a very practical command that involves some very practical actions and activities in our daily lives. But those actions and activities can make an eternal difference in their lives, if by those actions, they see the love of God in us, and are drawn to Him.

The Apostle Paul said in 1 Corinthians 13:4-7:

"Love does not give up. Love is kind. Love is not jealous. Love does not put itself up as being important. Love has no pride. Love does not do the wrong thing. Love never thinks of itself. Love does not get angry. Love does not remember the suffering that comes from being hurt by someone. Love is not happy with sin. Love is happy with the truth. Love takes everything that comes without giving up. Love believes all things. Love hopes for all things. Love keeps all things. Love never comes to an end." (Living Bible, paraphrased)

In Romans 13:10, the Apostle Paul said *"Love worketh no ill to his neighbor."* The word "ill" means "evil" - not only in evil actions, but in evil thinking. Consider that verse alongside of Proverbs 3:27-29 *"Withhold no good from them to whom it is due, when it is in the power of thine hand to do it. Say not unto thy neighbor, go and come again, and tomorrow I will give, when thou hast it by thee. Devise not evil against thy neighbor, seeing he dwelleth securely by thee."* A person who truly loves his neighbor as Christ has commanded will not work evil by wishing them harm or bad luck or even just recompense for their actions, even if they are evil. But rather his actions will be the work of love, as the evidence of God's work of love in his own heart. If God's love has been shed abroad in our hearts, it will naturally spill over upon our neighbors. It will mean that we will be willing to do what is best for our neighbors, regardless of the cost or sacrifice it may require. For after all, that was the kind of love God lavished upon me!

But the second question here is, "who are our neighbors?" And the obvious answer would be those who live next door, across the street or down the road. Wherever you live, God wants you to be on mission for Him.

We have some other neighbors as well. Those students at school are your neighbors. Those employers and employees where you work are your neighbors. Those merchants with whom we do business; those spontaneous encounters we have with the people we meet while we are shopping; those we sit by as we travel on the bus or the plane, or those we spend time with in the elevators or at the lunch counter, or those we speak to as we are walking to and from – these are our neighbors.

God has put us in our place of employment, not just to make an income, but to make an impact for eternity; to live our lives in such a way that others would see Jesus in us and ask for the reason we have such hope. God puts students in schools, not just to be students of knowledge, but as billboards for His truth; to live their lives in such a way that it would set them apart from the crowd, yet not too far away to help others find the Lord, if they should ask.

God prepares these divine encounters for us with people whom we may never see again. But we are commanded and commissioned to use those few seconds, those few moments, or perhaps those few hours to make an impact for eternity upon their hearts, by our demonstration of the love of God that we claim has made a difference in our own hearts.

The problem is that the majority of Christians are living by what they have always heard to be the golden rule, which says *"Do unto others as you would have them do unto you."* (Matthew 6:12) But, in John 13:34-35, **Jesus gave us a new commandment that we might call the "platinum" rule,** which says, *"Love one another AS I HAVE LOVED YOU."* (Emphasis mine) We are to do unto others as Jesus has done unto us. We are to lay down our lives for others as Jesus has given His life for us. And that is the key to real joy in our lives.

You say, "wait a minute! How can I be full of joy if I give up my life for others?" That is the paradox of true discipleship. The Christian life is totally opposite from the world. In Matthew 10:39, Jesus told His disciples *"He that findeth his life shall lose it. And he that loseth his life for my sake shall find it."* If someone lives their life just to satisfy his own selfish desires, and he is never concerned about anyone or anything else, what will he have when he comes to the end of his life? No matter how much he may accumulate, achieve or accomplish, it is for naught, and he will leave it all behind. But if he invests the days of his life helping others, not only will he be a blessing to others, but in so doing he too will be blessed, in this life, and in that life to come. **A person who closes their fist, holding on to what he has, can't receive any more, and what he has will rot and ruin in his hand. But a person who opens his hands and gives away what he has, according to the pattern of our Lord, will find fresh blessings and new mercies every morning, as well as abundant treasures awaiting him in heaven.**

It is ironic that the business world is returning to "personal service" in order to win new customers, while many Christians seem to be stuck on putting themselves first, and the contemporary model of the church seems to not only support, but enable that kind of selfishness. That's why there is so much apathy and boredom in the church today; there is no call for personal sacrifice; no challenge to get personally involved in the lives of people; no encouragement toward an outward expression of their faith. The whole focus seems to be on the upward beam of the cross, which is their worship of God, and even that seems to be for selfish motives. But we must remember, the two crossbeams that held the arms and hands of our Lord gave us a vivid demonstration of His love for lost mankind. And if that same Christ is truly alive in us, we will have the same compassion for the lost, and the same passion to see them saved.

But there is no sense of urgency about evangelism or fulfilling the great commission in the church today, whether it is an old established church that is locked in its traditions, or a new contemporary church that is following the fads of man. In so many words, those churches are telling lost people, if they want to come to Jesus they can find their own way. But that is not the way of our Lord, who gave Himself as a sacrifice for our sins.

But not only is there a command to be obeyed and a commission to be accepted, there is a commitment to be fulfilled. Jesus said our expressed love for God and our expressed love for man is the ultimate purpose behind all of scripture. This is, perhaps, the most overlooked emphasis of what Jesus said. He said the validation of all scripture "hangs" on our love for God and our love for our neighbor. In other words, whether or not we convince the unbelieving world of the truth of God's Word depends upon our love for God, as evidenced by our devotion to Him and our worship of Him, as well as our love for our neighbor, as evidenced by our attitude and actions toward them.

In 1 John 4:20-21, the beloved Apostle said a man proves he truly loves God when he truly loves his neighbor. *"If a man say, I love God, and hateth his brother, he is a liar; for he that loveth not his brother whom he hath seen, how can he love God whom he hath not seen? And this commandment have we from him, that he who loveth God loveth his brother also."* **So, when will we know that we have fulfilled our commitment to love our neighbors? When we love them the same way we want our Lord to love us!**

I cannot remember where I heard this story, but it made an indelible mark upon my heart. So much so, that as I came to the close of this chapter, I was reminded of it again. It was said, that whenever the emperors of Rome wanted to gratify the desires of their citizens gathered in those great amphitheaters to watch some sporting event, or to watch a play, or to listen to some great oratory, they would issue an order that sweet perfumes be released into the crowds. Giant vessels were unsealed and the sweet aroma of herbs soaked in oil and spices would instantly fill the air. Those giant jars were there all the time, and people passed by them day after day. But no one knew why the jars were there, nor were they affected by their contents until they were opened.

Our lives are like those sealed jars. God has put us in the world as vessels of His love, and He has commanded us to unseal our hearts and let the sweet aroma of His ever-lasting, unconditional and sacrificial love fill the air, replacing the stench of bitterness, hatred and self-centeredness that is in the world today, even among those who claim to be Christians. For unless we allow the aroma of His love to flow through us, no one will know why we are here, or be affected by our lives. Our witness will be worthless! Our lives, no matter how temporally successful, will have been wasted in the wanton pursuit of vain glory, instead of the glory of God. Our worship, no matter how exciting, vibrant, and culturally relevant, will be worthless, because it will not make any difference in our lives, or in our world, once we leave the four walls of the church building. Our works, regardless of how effective and helpful to the cause of

Christ, or to the lives of others, will be worthless, because our motives are not pure.

In 1 Corinthians 13:1, the Apostle Paul said, those who do what they do for the Lord, without the pure motive of love, *"become as sounding brass or a tinkling cymbal."* With all due respect to those church fellowships where the truth is being spoken in love, as far as the effectiveness of the church as a whole upon our sin-sick society, it is but "sounding brass, or the tink, tink, tinkling of a child's cymbal!" And quite frankly, not only is it not making any difference in the world, it's becoming quite annoying to the world, and they are telling us, in so many words, "be quiet!"

A wicked, hateful, divided world waits and wants to be touched by the love of God. God has commanded us to love them! Will you accept His commission to be a lover, even among the lost? Will you make your commitment to be that channel of God's love into the lives of others, even to those who are enemies of the cross? **The greatest argument for the truth of Christianity is a loving Christian! It wins every time!**

CHAPTER FOUR

The Raising Of the Standard In Our Love for the Church

I spend about forty hours each week comparing the moral condition of our world with what God has said in His Word, as well as the lack of influence the church is having upon our society. Were it not for the grace of God, the intensity of my agony would be more than I could stand. The leaders of the world, including our own President, are saying that **the only power that can cleanse us from this filth of sin, and restore us to some sense of reasonableness and sanity, is a fresh outpouring of the Holy Spirit upon God's people.** And, according to Holy Scripture, the primary way that power would be manifested is through the local Church: The Body of Christ.

However, **on any given Sunday, the majority of Christians will not even attend church;** much less get involved in some position of responsibility to help make a difference in anyone's life. Today, many people who call themselves Christians don't see the need to be a member of any church. They are just "regular visitors," folks who attend when the church is doing something that appeals to them or that meets their needs, but never really plugging in to help meet the needs of others. They may even have their names on the roll in several churches, even of several denominations, but there is no real commitment to a particular church body, or to a statement of faith of what they truly believe about Jesus.

The Bible is very clear about the purpose of the local church and the need for Christians to be committed to a body of believers. The church is the Body of Christ in the world today. It is the channel through which God has ordained for the gospel to be proclaimed, and for His love to be revealed to the world. **Therefore, what a person "thinks" of the church is actually what he thinks of Christ.** One cannot love Christ without loving the church, because it is not just an organization or a denomination, it is the Body of the living Christ!

One of my dearest pastor friends was Dr. Ed Vallowe, an evangelist who preached in more than 1000 different churches in his sixty years of ministry. In one of his sermons, Dr. Vallowe estimated that less than 10% of church attenders are truly saved. He clarified his remarks by saying, while that statement could not be said of any single church, when you counted those who are attending churches based upon false doctrine who aren't saved, plus those who have their names on a church roll of a Bible believing church, but never attend, the faithful few get fewer and fewer. Personally, I think he is correct.

In a pastor's seminar, the great expository preacher, Dr. Stephen Olford, who also is now in heaven sitting at the feet of Jesus, said today's church is filled with what he termed *"evangelical humanists!"* He described them as those who worship their own concept of Christ, rather than the Christ of the Bible. But, he said, even their faith is based upon what they want the Lord to do for them, rather than what God may be calling them to do for Him. In other words, they want God on their terms and not His.

I believe the warning of Hebrews 10:22-25 needs to be implanted into the heart of every true Christian:

"Let us draw near with a true heart in full assurance of faith, having our hearts sprinkled from an evil conscience, and our bodies washed with pure water. Let us hold fast the profession of our faith without wavering. And let us consider one another to provoke unto love and to good works; not forsaking the assembling of ourselves together as the manner of some is; but exhorting one another; and so much the more, as ye see the day approaching."

I'm sure you would agree that, if there ever was a day when every believer needs to be assembled together in the church-house, it is today. If there ever was a day when the church-house needs to be filled and overflowing, it is today. If there ever was a day when Christians need to be united together, lifting high the royal banner of the cross of Christ, most assuredly it is today! And yet, as it has already been documented in the earlier chapters of this book, **overall church attendance is down, and it is continuing to fall, even now in the mega-churches, those with over 5000 in regular attendance.**

The Bible teaches, and human experience confirms, that man was created for the expressed purpose of worshiping God. The first question in the Westminster Catechism asks, **"What is the chief end of man?" The answer given is, "the chief end of man is to glorify God and to enjoy Him forever!"**

God graced us with a desire to worship – it is like a void in our hearts that can only be filled with God Himself. That desire to worship is God's homing device, that sense of need that calls man back to his maker. Man will never be satisfied until he finds the object of his worship, which is the true and living God. Without that true worship of God, man will degenerate and develop animalistic tendencies, such as we see today in man's gross, indecent and immoral behavior. **The bottom line is, man will try to fill that void by worshiping the god of his own making, or he will worship the God who made him, but worship he will.**

God designed the soul to function on a regular diet of truth, worship and ministry. If that soul is forsaken by a lack of Bible study, or a lack of genuine, God-focused worship, or even a lack of ministry to others, it begins to lose its capacity for God. The mind becomes saturated with so many lies that it has no capacity for truth, and therefore for God. The conscience becomes so saturated with sin that there is no sense of shame or guilt over any kind of immoral behavior. And the emotions become so engrossed and entangled with all kind of feelings, that the person becomes confused about how they feel. They are no longer able to discern what true love is, or experience real joy.

Without that true worship of God, the soul becomes desperately miserable, incapable of being fully satisfied with anything or anyone. And unless that soul is regenerated by the Holy Spirit, and is born again, it begins to die spiritually. If that process continues, it will soon reach the point where, as Paul says in Romans 1:21-32, God will *"give them over to a reprobate mind; to uncleanness, and to vile affections."* In other words, they begin to act like mere animals, such as we see in man's immoral behavior today. That is why we need to gather together every Lord's day and worship Him. **The true worship of God not only cleans our heart of all sin, it also restores real joy to our soul.**

Psychologists tell us that a habit is formed in about twenty-one days. When a believer is absent from church just one Sunday that is thirteen days apart from the fellowship and support of God's people. Make that two consecutive Sundays and it jumps to twenty days apart from the spiritually energizing experience of corporate worship, and a habit is about to be formed. According to some of the "de-churched" folks I interviewed, the third Sunday to be absent becomes easier, and the next even easier, and so forth, because the old habit of going to church on Sunday has been broken, and a new habit of not attending has been made.

If that person is an unbeliever, pretty soon the conscience will be so seared that they won't even be bothered with it any more. And, unless there is some catastrophic event that draws them back to the Lord, they may never darken the door of the church again. But if that person is a true believer, there will be a nagging feeling inside, telling them they are missing something in their life. Just like a hunger pain tells us it is time to eat, **there will be a deep gnawing in the soul of every true believer that is away from the warm fires of worship, telling us that we need to be with God's people; we need to worship God**. We need to be in church! That is God's way of calling us back to Himself! That is God's way of calling us back to worship, not because He needs it, but because we do!

Twice in my ministry career, Linda and I have been without a church home for a season. During those times while we waited for God to reveal our next assignment, we attended several churches, heard some good singing and good preaching, and on some Sundays I was able to fill a vacant pulpit. But what we missed most was our time of worship with our own church family.

I missed looking out and seeing the same folks sitting in the same places every Sunday. I missed walking into the waters of baptism with those who had been saved. I missed hearing familiar voices praising the Lord with all of their heart; and knowing they meant every word they were singing. I missed looking at those at the altar during prayer time, knowing the heart-deep needs of those who were on their knees and drenched in tears.

I missed little children running up to me and reaching out for a hug. I missed young people asking me how they could know the will of God on a certain matter. I missed hearing what God had been doing in the lives of the people as I greeted them with a warm handshake, or often a great big hug. I missed being in the pulpit and feeding the sheep from the Word of God, praying that it would touch the lives of those who had come to hear a word from Him.

Linda missed the challenge of singing in the choir and saying "amen" at every good point in my sermon. She missed holding the babies, teaching the toddlers, answering the questions of a pregnant mom or listening to the hurting heart of a teenage girl. She missed preparing meals and snacks for groups we met with, or planning the annual ladies prayer retreats. Looking so young, but being so "mature," Linda has a special way with senior adults; perhaps the most overlooked age group in the church. At first, she had to look them up to let them know she was glad to see them, and they were quite surprised to know that anyone cared. But it wasn't long until they began to expect that kind of attention. They missed it when she was not there, and so did she.

By God's grace, both of us grew up in churches that were alive with worship. Linda had sixteen years of perfect attendance in church, and would have had more, probably, if she had not married me. In most of the churches where we have served, we both have experienced the joy and blessing of God-focused worship, where the majority of people came expecting to meet God, expecting to hear from Him through the preaching of His Word, and prepared to give Him the glory and honor due His holy name.

We have also served in some churches where the time of worship was more calculated; structured for live television. While the Pastor was always on target as far as the preaching, there was tension about the timing of the services that often squelched the freedom of the Holy Spirit. Other services we have attended have been cold, indifferent, perfunctory and with no sense of God's presence. Still others have been so unorganized and flippant that we left feeling like it had been a royal waste of time. Our hearts hurt even more as we wondered how a holy God felt about what He had heard!

Since the day God radically changed our lives, "church" has become a priority for us. The truth is Linda and I live for the day when we can worship together with our new family of faith once again. Each time we have left a church, even though we knew it was God's will, it was like going through the death of a loved one. The pain of separation was often more than we could bear. And even though we know that God puts us where He wants us for a reason and a season, we long for that day when we can go to our own church and begin to build those kinds of relationships again.

Do you feel that way about being in your church on Sunday? **Is there a hunger in your heart to be with the family of God every Sunday?** If there is, you can know that you are a child of God, and that God is calling you to do what He designed you to do: to worship Him in spirit and in truth. If not, perhaps you need to review your salvation experience to make sure you have been truly born again.

Everyone is worshipping their god on the Lord's Day. Some are worshiping themselves, because they see this as their day to rest. Some are worshiping the twin gods of nature and pleasure. To them it is a holiday, not a holy day. Some are worshipping the gods of success, using their "off day" to improve their own skills so they can glorify themselves instead of the God of all glory. Others spend the day catching up on past work, so they can take pride in themselves for getting their work done. Some are worshiping the god of mammon because they think money will supply all of their needs, wants and desires.

But the true Christian, the one who has been truly born again by the Holy Spirit of God, will be in worship in the Lord's house on the Lord's Day. In fact, there is nothing that can keep a true believer from attending worship, unless his love for the Lord grows cold, or his physical condition prohibits it. No, you don't have to attend church to be saved. But if you are saved, nothing can keep you from attending church, because God's call to be saved is also the call to worship Him!

Note: (A deeper development of the subject of worship will be addressed in a later chapter)

But not only is there a call to worship in the church, there is also a call to be a witness, both in and through the church. The words "hold fast" describe the soldier who fearlessly carries the banner right into the heat of battle, raising it even higher as he marches onward; not considering the danger he is facing, but committed to the victory he has been promised, if he marches on. As Christians, we are to hold fast to our confession of faith in Jesus Christ. We are to lift high His royal banner; not considering the hostility we will receive from others by our Christian witness.

And what is that confession of faith we are to hold on to? Paul outlined it in 1 Corinthians 15:3-4: *"Christ died for our sins, according to the scriptures; and He was buried and that He rose again the third day, according to the scriptures."* **Whatever else the church stands for, or against, this is the confession of faith that sets us apart as Christians.** It is not up for discussion, debate, alteration or explanation. This is the statement of our Christian faith, and what we must believe in order to be saved.

But as we look at the involvement of today's church in society, is our Christian witness to the world based upon *the Savior whom we confess, or that worldly sin we so detest*?

In other words, does the world know the church today by our confession of faith in Christ, or by our protest against the sins of the world? The answer is obvious.

The world's impression of the church today is not too positive. Christians are viewed as a bunch of homophobic dunces who are stuck in the dark ages, who have to use God for a crutch to get through life, and who want to force their way of life upon everyone. Not only do they see us as a hindrance to their personal freedoms, but they also see us as being involved in places we do not belong, such as politics, public education, the private lives of people, health care and other issues where they reject our moral absolutes. And while the media elite give "church attendance" a nod, as being the nice and moral thing to do on Sunday, they actually see no point in it because they see no power from it. Again, they see us as being more interested in keeping the Ten Commandments posted on the courthouse walls then we are in making sure they are inscribed upon our hearts, or just obeyed by those who claim to believe in them, and have accepted them as a way of life.

There are many who may not know that the first public schools, colleges, universities and graduate schools were started by Christians who saw the need for quality education. There are many who may not know that the first hospitals and nursing home, children's homes and retirement homes were started by Christians who saw the need to help the hurting. There are those who have never been told that the Sunday School was started by a man who saw the need to get abandoned children off the street, give them a little food, show them love, and teach them about the love of God. There are those who have never heard of the thousands of missionaries who have sacrificed their lives in ministry to those whom others would never even bother with, in the slums and ghettos of America, and in the villages and disease-infected camps in nations and with names we cannot pronounce.

There are those who never stop to consider how many lives have been saved, how many families have been fed, how many minds have been trained, or how many generations have been affected by the ministry of the local church. Many times, it has been the witness of Christians that has prevented nations from going to war with other nations. And Christians were there when the wars were over to help the innocent victims.

There are those who never hear of the help that is given by Christians, even this very day, to people around the world, as well as here at home, when disaster strikes. Billions of dollars in food, clothing and other kinds of relief is provided to these hurting people, with absolutely no strings attached. Billions of hours in medical aid, educational help and emotional assistance are given to those who are hurting and helpless. In my own denomination, disaster relief teams are on 24-hour alert, with trucks packed and ready for food preparation, sanitation and mobile communication.

Recently, a missionary reported that the Muslim people in Indonesia were taking notice of what Christians had done for them in the aftermath of the tsunami. He said the people had been taught that the Muslims were their friends and the Christians were their enemies. *"But,"* the man asked, *"if the Christians were their enemies, why were they there, doing the dirty, filthy, and often dangerous jobs to help them that no one else would or could do? And if the Muslims were their friends, why weren't they there at all?"*

No, my friend, **the world isn't taking notice of our Christian witness today because we have been marching under the wrong banner**. Christianity is not a political party out to change the world at the ballot box. Christianity is not an entertainment industry out to attract the world with amateur theatre and worldly music. Christianity is not a philosophy of life that makes its followers live in Christian homes, in Christian neighborhoods, and drive Christian cars and shop in Christian stores and only listen to Christian radio or watch Christian TV. Christianity is not even a religion with a creed to be believed, or with laws to be obeyed, or an order of worship to be followed. True Christianity is not a way of life that was written in our constitution or guaranteed in our nations' bill of rights. Christianity did not begin 200 years ago when Christian men stepped on Plymouth Rock and claimed this as a God blessed nation! Christianity began 2000 years ago when the Rock of all ages hung between two thieves, on a cruel cross, and gave His life as a sacrifice for the sins of every man. And Christianity has grown through the blood of those who believed in that Savior and who have served Him as their Lord. And so it continues to grow today.

The lost people of the world will not be saved by our hatred of sin, but their hearts may be changed by our love for the Lord Jesus Christ, and the burden He gives us to witness to them about His love for them. And I believe **the greatest, and perhaps the most effective witness we can have in the world today is our regular attendance in church every Lord's Day**, worshiping the true and living God with other believers.

Our lost neighbors need to see us driving or walking to church every Sunday morning, rain or shine. They may not know what we believe or why we believe it, but at least they know we are serious about it, and that we are committed to it. Unbelievers need to God's house filled and overflowing every Sunday as they drive by on their way to worship their god. They need to wonder what is going on in our place of worship that would draw such a crowd, and what they might be missing by not being there themselves. Perhaps more importantly, they need to see the difference that kind of commitment to worship has made, and continues to make in our lives.

But not only is there a call to Christian worship and a call to Christian witness, there is also a call to Christian

welfare. We are to assume responsibility for each other as equal members of the family of God. Two activities are mentioned in this verse, (Hebrews 10:22-25) we are to consider one another, and we are to exhort one another.

To consider one another means more than to just think about each other occasionally, or greet each other when we meet on Sunday. It means to consider how we might be able to minister to each other in some way, or to motivate each other to love and good works. It means there will always be those in the church who will need a little encouragement, a little extra consideration and perhaps even motivation. Records reveal that the average church member attends about twice a month, and rarely takes a position of leadership or responsibility. Over half of the people on the church rolls hardly ever attend. But our ministry to them should never be to neglect them, as they have, and continue to neglect the church family. But our responsibility is to *consider* how we might be able to restore them to the body, which leads to the second activity, which is to exhort one another.

To exhort one another means we challenge each other to not forsake the assembling of ourselves together. That means we have a mutual responsibility for the spiritual welfare of each church member, and an obligation to exhort each other to not abandon God's call for us to assemble ourselves together in the Lord's house on the Lord's Day. Remember, Jesus said the world would know that we are Christians by our love for one another. A loving call, a personal note, a timely visit, a deed of kindness, or a special gift on their special day might just be the act of exhortation a person needs to remind them of their responsibility to the church family.

The main reason people give for leaving a church is that they "perceive" no one really cares about them. Whether that is true or not, it is their perception. And unless that perception is corrected by our loving exhortation, it will soon become reality. Take a good concordance and review the "one-another's" in Paul's letters to the churches.

We have a tremendous responsibility to one another in the Body of Christ. If the world doesn't see that love manifested in the Church, where will they see it manifested at all?

There are many people who have their names on a church roll, having made a confession of their faith in Jesus Christ, and having made a commitment to serve Him as Lord, but who have renounced their confession, reneged on their commitment to Christ, and returned to worship their former gods. It is what Paul said would happen in the last days of the church age. It is called apostasy, the time when many, many people will turn away from the truth faith, as outlined in the Bible, and return to the fables and myths of the religions of the world. We are seeing that today, even in the evangelical church.

It is also my opinion that even many churches have been enticed into this false doctrine by their desires for fame and recognition. Just as Satan promised such vain-glory to Jesus if He would only follow his pathway, I believe many churches have fallen victim to such deception today, because they did not have the spiritual foundation sufficient to resist Satan's promise of great attendance, recognition, prestige, honor and financial reward. Many of the "de-churched" have left these churches, not because they left their first love for the Lord, and not because they have fallen away from the true faith, but because their church has, and they have no place to go. This is the one issue that is breaking my heart!

We must raise the standard in our love for the church, by renewing our commitment to the Lordship of Christ, and by determining to be in the Lord's house on the Lord's Day, and to encourage others to do the same. **What does it say to an unbeliever when they see someone who has professed to be a believer not attending church on Sunday?**

There is sufficient evidence in the Bible for me to conclude that the second coming of Christ will be on a Sunday, the Lord's Day! (1 Thessalonians 5:2, 2 Thessalonians 2:2, 2 Peter 3:10) Wouldn't it be wonderful if the rapture of the Church occurred on the Lord's Day? All of God's people would be gathered in our respective houses of worship, singing praises unto His holy Name, hearing the preaching of His Word, and then be ushered right into His presence with His praises on our lips and His truth implanted in our hearts. Can I be sure of that? No! But can you be sure that it won't happen on a Sunday? Should the Lord call for His Church next Sunday morning, will you be present and ready?

The 19th century British pastor Charles Haddon Spurgeon called the local church *"the dearest place on Earth."* The Lord designed the church to serve as a little colony of heaven on earth; a place for believers to gather and to be encouraged by the teachings of God's Word and the fellowship of the saints; a place where our covenant with God can be renewed through the proclamation of God's Word, the administration of the Lord's Supper and baptism; a place of retreat from the unholiness of the world and a place where there is respect for the holiness of God. Do you have such a view of your church?

One of the greatest joys Linda and I ever had was to lead a group of people on a tour of the beautiful land of Israel. From the Golan Heights near Lebanon to the Dead Sea near Jordan, and many places in between, we traveled over 800 miles by bus, and many miles on foot, as we followed the footsteps of Jesus from His birthplace in Bethlehem to the place of His death at Calvary, and then to the empty tomb. What took Jesus more than three years to travel; we tried to do it in about a week. Yet, even in this small amount of time, the true significance of each location is forever embedded in our minds and will be a precious memory that will forever change the way we read and understand the Bible.

Something happened on one of our tours that we will never forget. After traveling through Galilee and visiting the sites of our Lord's earthly ministry, we drove the 90 miles down through the Jordan Valley to the city of Jericho. Then we turned west for the 15 mile ride to Jerusalem, on that same road that Jesus traveled 2000 years ago. Just about dusk we drove up the eastern side of the Mount of Olives and through the winding streets of East Jerusalem. We were listening to a tape of John Starnes singing "The Holy City." As we topped the ridge of the Mount of Olives, John began his final chorus: *"Jerusalem, Jerusalem, lift up your voice and sing! Hoshanna, in the highest. Hoshanna to the King!* And right before our very eyes was the old city – Jerusalem – the beautiful city of God. That was a sight to behold. It was so breathtaking, we didn't know whether to applaud or cry, so we did both.

The city of Zion was all aglow from the evening sun shining against the beautiful sandstone buildings. Even the golden dome of the Moslem Mosque, where the Moslems worship the prophet Mohammed, added its own beauty to that sacred city. And I wondered how it must have looked to Jesus when He arrived at that same spot 2000 years earlier, ready to give His life as a ransom for our sins.

You see, we don't understand the love the Jew has for the city of Jerusalem. To the Jew, Jerusalem is like a Holy Place within the Holy Land. To the Jew, Jerusalem is the city of peace. For thousands of years, Jerusalem was the site of their temple, which was not only the dwelling place of God, but the gathering place for all of God's people. Even in the day of Jesus, Jews from around the world made their annual visit to Jerusalem for the Feast of Passover. And even though the temple is no longer there, Jews by the thousands go to the Wailing Wall every day, just to be as near to that site where their temple was, and where the new temple will one day be restored. And there they pray to the God of Abraham, Isaac, and Jacob for their restoration as a nation, and as the people of God.

Just as there is a special place in our hearts for our hometown, there is a deep hunger in the heart of every Jew to be near his homeland, the City of Jerusalem. To them, and to millions of Christians, Jerusalem is still the city of God. No, we don't understand the desire that God has placed in the heart of every Jewish person to be near Jerusalem, but we should.

An artist captured that sentiment in a beautiful painting I hope to possess one day. It describes the anticipation of the people as they are making their way toward the city of Jerusalem for a time of celebration. Some are on camel, others on donkeys, and others are walking hurriedly toward that city. The artist illustrated their joy and excitement as they top the last hill and see the walls of that Holy City just ahead. Only a few more minutes and they will be inside the gates and in the security of its walls. And some seem to be breaking out into a run so they will not be the last ones to arrive.

How wonderful it would be if we had that same attitude toward our place of worship. How wonderful it would be if we had the same excitement about the place that has been set aside for our worship as the Jew has about Jerusalem. How wonderful it would be if we had the same excitement about seeing the first sight of that steeple, or that small cross on the top of the sanctuary, or just the roof line of the building, as the Jews had about seeing the watchtowers on the walls of Jerusalem. **How wonderful it would be if we had the same longing in our heart to be in our place of worship on the Lord's Day as the Jew has in his heart every day.** How wonderful it would be if, when people turned the corner and saw our church facilities, they could say the same thing as we did when we saw the old city of

Jerusalem – now there is a sight to behold.

In Psalm 122, King David wrote these challenging words: *"I was glad when they said unto me, let us go into the house of the Lord. Our feet shall stand within thy gates, O Jerusalem. Peace be within thy walls, and prosperity within thy palaces."* I believe we must raise the standard of our love for the church facility as much as for the church body. **For our attitude toward the place where we worship is a reflection of our heart for the One we worship. And the lost world is watching!**

CHAPTER FIVE

The Raising Of the Standard In Our Worship of God

Part One: God's Desire For Worship

As we approach this serious and sensitive subject of worship, I believe it would be of benefit to review the basic assertion of this book. It is scripturally clear that the Lord left His church on earth to be His witnesses to the world. (Matthew 28:18-20, Acts 1:8) He said we are to be as lights, shining brightly against the darkness of sin, and our righteous lives should be as salt, preserving society from total decay.(Matthew 5:13-16) The church is the Lord's standard bearer in the world, and we are to lift high His royal banner!

But as we near the end of the last days of the church age, it is also very painfully clear that the lights of the church have grown dim. Comfort, compromise, complacency, and conformity have replaced convictions, commitment, doctrinal consistency, and Biblical certainty. **Rather than going to the world with a clear message of the cross of Christ, and its effect upon our lives, the church is adjusting its ministries to attract the world to itself.** Therefore, we are giving the world an "uncertain sound," as the Apostle Paul referred to in 1 Corinthians 14:7-8. And, as he said in verse 23 of that same passage, rather than the unbelievers and unlearned being convicted of their sin and convinced of their need for Christ, they think "(we) *are mad!*"

Likewise, the salt of the church has all but lost its savor, meaning its power of influence. Rather than being in the world, and yet not of it, many Christians have allowed the world to squeeze them into its mold. **Most Christians have decided to acquiesce with society rather than to incur the ridicule and persecution for being different from society.** Therefore, by not being willing to be different, Christians are not making any significant difference in the values and virtues of our world today. The world delights to point out the sins and shortcomings of those high-profile people who have professed their faith in Jesus Christ, and who brag about being "born again!" The underlying allegation is that being a "born again Christian" makes no difference; "It" doesn't work!

That is why we must raise the standard of our Lord Jesus Christ in the church. The enemy is coming in like a flood, and from various directions and sources. He is rising up against every truth, every value, and every virtue, everything you and I hold dear, including the very validity of our faith in God. **Our children and our grandchildren are being drenched in a sea of lies and half-truths that are affecting their concept of life, their value of life, and that may determine the location of their eternal life**. And the only answer to the lies of the world is for Jesus Christ to be lifted up once again as the Way, the Truth, and the Life, just as He said He was in John 14:6.

One of the main areas where the church must lift up the standard is in the area of worship. In every interview I have had with a prospective church, this was one of, if not the main issue of concern. In one church it was the main topic of a two-hour question and answer session with the church body. In many cases, it was also the cause of the vacancy in the pulpit as their former pastor had fallen victim to the "worship wars" in one way or the other. In fact, in those instances, I cannot remember being asked about my doctrines, my theology, whether I was a Calvinist or Armenian, whether I believed in the "pre – post – or mid" – tribulation rapture, or the "pre – post – or ah" – millennial return of Jesus Christ. But I have spent hours and hours in discussion, and outright debate over the issue of what would be allowed to take place in the time of corporate worship. **It is without a doubt the battleground in churches today, and Satan is using that battle to divide many families, many friends, and therefore to destroy many churches.**

From these interviews, I have concluded that **the main reason for this dilemma is the absence of a clear, biblical definition of the term worship.** If each of us wrote down our definition of worship, we probably would have as many different answers as we have readers, and most likely each answer would include some of the same things, such as praise, prayer and preaching, because that is what most of us have grown up believing.

But the division comes as to what kind of music should be used in the worship service, and what instruments should be played? What is acceptable prayer? Who should be allowed to pray? Whom, or what should we be praying for? What kind of preaching should the preacher preach, for how long, and to whom, and for what purpose?

While it is true that worship may include all of those things, the fact is, one can do all of those things, customized according to tastes and talent, and not genuinely worship God. Every religion has its praise, its prayers and its proclamation. Even the world has its music, its mediums and its messages for and from the gods of this world, and they worship them religiously, and support them faithfully.

Today, we are more concerned about the events within the worship service, rather than the true purpose for which we are gathered. **The missing ingredient in much of modern worship today, whether it is contemporary or traditional, liturgical or free-spirit is our lack of reverence and respect for the holiness of God**. Just going through the motions and activities of a worship service without the right heart motive is not true biblical worship. According to Jesus, it is narcissistic vanity and blatant hypocrisy of the highest order. *"Ye hypocrites, well did Isaiah prophesy of you, saying, this people draweth nigh unto me with their lips; but their heart is far from me. But in vain they do worship me, teaching for doctrines the commandments of men."* (Matthew 15:7-9)

Jesus told the woman at the well, *"The hour cometh, when true worshipers shall worship the Father in SPIRIT AND IN TRUTH, for the Father seeketh such to worship Him. God is Spirit and those that worship Him MUST worship Him in SPIRIT AND IN TRUTH."* (John 4:23, Emphasis mine) "Spirit" and "Truth" have to do with the motive and intent of our heart, not the actions of our hands or our heads.

As we have stated before, apart from the grace of God, man would have no desire to worship God at all – what can a dead man do to worship God? (Ephesians 2:1-10) But as a result of the quickening of the Holy Spirit, God gave us the desire to worship Him; to express our thanks unto Him, not only for delivering us from eternal death and giving us eternal life, but in showing us how to have purpose and meaning in this earthly life, which includes returning unto God all the praise, the glory, the adoration and the love He rightly deserves. But, having that intrinsic desire to worship, we must also remember that God has already determined how He must be worshiped.

God desires us to worship Him in spirit! When God breathed into Adam's lifeless body, man became a living soul. That breath was the Holy Spirit of God! When we are born again, we are indwelt and empowered by the Holy Spirit; enabled to do whatever the Lord calls us to do for His glory and His honor. It is the work of the Holy Spirit to keep us saved until we are in the Lord's presence and to use the circumstances of our lives to conform us to the image of Jesus Christ. (Romans 8:28-29)

I believe the Bible illustrates at least three different types or kinds of worship.

- **There is a need for personal worship** – that daily quiet time with the Lord, without which the true believer will never fully become mature in his faith or approved as a workman who needeth not to be ashamed. The Lord Jesus modeled this kind of worship for us as we are told in Mark 1:35: *"And in the morning, rising up a great while before day, he went out, and departed into a solitary place, and there prayed."* If He, being God of very God, Himself, yet on earth as man of very man, thought it necessary to spend those early morning hours on His face before the Father, then how can we dare to do any less. Years ago, I did my own survey of those men whom God had used in a mighty way, those whose ministry, even though they had been physically dead for years, was still having an effect on the lives of Christians today. The one common denominator between all of these men was that they followed our Lord's pattern in regard to personal worship – they invested hours each day before the Lord in private devotions and personal prayer, and God rewarded them publicly. (See Matthew 6:4) There is no substitute for personal worship; that time where we come before Him, confess our sins, and renew our covenant with Him, according to His Word.

- **There is a need for family worship** – that time each day, when the family gathers at some place in the home, sings unto the Lord, shares their prayer requests and listens to the teachings of the Word of God. While we will deal with this more thoroughly in a later chapter, let me be very clear that just as God has not altered His exhortation that His people worship Him corporately, as we will see next, neither has He changed His plan regarding family worship. The husband/father is the spiritual head of each family, and as such, he has the God-ordained responsibility for the spiritual development of his family. And one day, he will give an account unto God for this awesome responsibility. Neither personal worship, nor corporate worship is a substitute for family worship, and it is needed in our homes today more than ever.

- **There is a need for corporate worship** – that time each week when we gather with other believers in that place that has been set aside for worship and we lift our hearts and voices in praise, adoration, confession and exaltation to the One who has called us to Himself, even Jesus Christ our Lord, we listen intently to the proclamation of the Word of God, and we bring unto Him an offering; a sacrifice that is worthy of His Holy Name, as an indication to Him that we recognize Him as the source of our every blessing. These times with God's people are, as the song writer said it, a "foretaste of glory divine," dress rehearsals, if you will, for that day which is quickly coming when all the saints of all the ages will gather around the throne of God and worship the Lamb forever and forever. Sadly, in many churches, the Lord's Day has been filled with everything but genuine worship; evangelistic crusades, lectures on morality, political rallies, concerts or other major musical productions, or sermon-seminars on a variety of subjects related to everyday life and living. A.W. Tozer was absolutely right when he said the missing jewel in today's church is worship; genuine, biblical worship, and unfortunately, the majority of the people in the evangelical church today have never experienced true worship, and therefore they do not know what they are missing. As you will read in the other chapters of this book, this corporate gathering of believers is not only of great benefit to the believer in terms of accountability, encouragement and biblical training, but it is also the most effective way of witnessing to the rest of the world Who we worship and why. That is the real heart burden behind the writing of this book.

But whether it is in our time of personal, family or corporate worship, **when we allow the Holy Spirit within us to draw us so near to the heart of God that there is a level of intimacy and oneness between us that is deeper than words can express, that is when we can say we have truly worshiped.** When we can sense the presence of God so much so, that we are, at least to some degree, oblivious, or at least immune to others who may be around us, we can say we have truly worshiped. When we allow the Holy Spirit absolute freedom to convict, to comfort, to encourage, to prompt, to teach, and to guide us into all truth, then we can say we have truly worshiped.

However, if in our time of corporate worship, our attention is upon the preacher, his appearance, his intellect, his eloquence, his mannerisms, his teachings, (and those could be positive or negative traits), instead of the One whom he is preaching about, and the truth he is trying to impart, our oneness with the Spirit has been broken, and we are not worshiping. Instead, we are listening to a message designed by man for our benefit, and no matter how many notes are written down on our paper, the truth will not be inscribed upon our hearts, because, unless it is God's Word, its just more good information.

Sadly, thousands gather in places of worship every Lord's day to listen to a man speak on various subjects of felt needs and human interests from the biblical perspective rather than to hear a preacher proclaim the whole counsel of Word of God. They attend a certain church because they like the preacher, or how he preaches or his opinions on certain issues. That may be fine for a special conference, but that isn't true, biblical worship!

Likewise, if our attention is upon the choir, the soloist, the organist, the pianist, the orchestra, or the music, rather than the One whom they are singing about, and the One to whom they are singing, then our worship is in not in the Spirit but in the flesh. If that is the case, then to some degree, we are being entertained by a performance rather than being led to truly worship God through the praise of His glory and His grace. (Ephesians 1:6) And the applause of the audience is apt to be more for the wonderful presentation of the music rather than true praise for our wonderful Lord.

Music is a gift from our Creator, and it is a wonderful medium through which the message of God's character and God's attributes can be delivered. But music is also the medium through which Satan, who was once in charge of all the praise of heaven, can capture our soul, our mind, our will and our emotions and therefore deceives us into believing that we are worshiping God, when we are really glorifying ourselves.

Martin Luther, the founder of the Lutheran Church, said the reason he began to write songs was to help his people learn the basic doctrines of the Christian faith, and to help them understand the deep theological concepts of salvation, redemption, sanctification and glorification. Luther, who influenced church music perhaps more than any other man, said *"next to the Word of God, music deserves the highest praise."* (*Give Praise to God,* Ryken, Thomas & Duncan, P&R Publishing Company, 2003) There is no doubt that this was the same motive of John and Charles Wesley, the founders of the Methodist Church, who wrote hundreds of hymns and choruses that are still being used today.

In Colossians 3:16-17, the Apostle Paul encouraged the people to *"let the word of Christ dwell within you, with all wisdom, teaching and admonishing one another with psalms and hymns and spiritual songs, singing with thankfulness in your hearts to God."*

In the Old Testament, the Jewish people used music not only to catalogue the history of their people, and God's interaction with them, but they also used it to teach their children about that history, and God's love for them. The Psalms are truly their songs of faith.

Music is a tool to help people conceptualize the old, old story, of Jesus and His love. Music is also one of the methods by which we can express our worship unto God. There are more than 6000 references to music in the Bible, and we know that singing is going to be one of our eternal activities. James Montgomery Boice, who in his last years of ministry began to address this crucial issue of music as it relates to worship, wrote*: "Music is a gift from God that allows us to express our deepest heart responses to God and his truth in meaningful and memorable ways. It is a case of our hearts joining with our minds to say yes, yes, yes to the truths we are embracing in our song."* (*Give Praise to God,* Ryken, Thomas & Duncan, P&R Publishing Company, 2003)

But if the music itself becomes more important, or more powerful, or more dramatic, or more attractive, or more appealing than the biblical message it was intended

to communicate, it has lost its place in true, biblical worship**. Again, sadly, this is what is offered in too many churches today as worship music.

If we are going to raise the standard in our worship of God, we must become more concerned about whether or not our worship music pleases God than we are about whether or not it appeals to man. For if the music itself, because of its beat or style, appeals to the lower nature of man, which all worldly music does, or if it attracts the attention or emotions of man to the music, rather than the message, then it may detract a person from truly worshiping God. The song may use Christian words, have a Christian theme, a great testimony, or an inspiring challenge, but if there is anything in that song or music that exalts itself above the worship of God, it is not fit for true biblical worship!

In other words, **if our theology does not dictate our worship music, then our worship music will dictate our theology**, and that is why we have seen such a lowering of the concept of God today, especially in the minds of our children and our youth. To a large degree, their understanding of God is being derived from a song, which is, at its best an extrapolation of a truth or a principle from the Bible, or at its worst, a personal testimony, which is very subjective and relative, rather than from the absolute, divinely inspired, infallible and inerrant Word of God.

I am encouraged to see some of those who were once strong proponents of "Christian Rock Music," now finally seeing the fallacy and futility of their folly, and turning in their trite logos for the true Logos! I say that with the utmost humility and meekness, for "but for the grace of God, there go I!" The first thirteen years of my adult life were spent behind a microphone, spinning records as a disc-jockey. I know the intrinsic, as well as the extrinsic power of music, and I have used music to convey every kind of message, sell every kind of item and to promote every kind of experience in life, and it worked. Advertisers and merchandisers and retailers know the power of music, which is why you hear it almost everywhere you go. Music is an attention getter! Music is a mood-setter! Music is a motivator! Music is an activator! Music is a powerful, powerful tool!

It was an invitation to participate in a musical team that attracted my wife and me back to the local church in 1972. But thank God, it was the testimonies we heard and the biblical discipleship we received from some of the team members that drew us back to the Lord, and to His Word. In 1974, God called me to leave that broadcasting career and to prepare for the ministry. During my studies, I served as Minister of Music in several churches and led many choirs and musical teams on tours. We used music as a tool to get the truth of the gospel into the minds of those who were singing it. In talking with several of those who were involved in those groups, they assured me that the music, or the presentation of the music, never became more important than the message, and it never detracted from the One we were singing about, and it never changed their concept of true worship.

The Greek word that is translated as "worship" in the New Testament is "proskuneo" which means to kiss, like a dog licking his master's hand; to prostrate oneself in homage, such as one would do in greeting a king; to bow and kiss his ring, his robe, or even his feet. That is quite a contrast when compared with the tawdry, gaudy, flashy, showy, and often flamboyant attitude in many worship services today, and not only by those who are singers and musicians, but by many preachers as well.

Watching some of them on television today, one wonders what the purpose of it all is. Certainly, God is not being worshiped by it, and lost man is not being impressed with the love of God or for his need for Christ by it, so the only conclusion is that it is for edification of those who are participating in the performance, or those who are watching it. But true worship is not the same as attending a concert or watching a presentation, or even participating in a seminar or conference on spiritual issues. **True worship is when we bow down before the Father in humble submission, recognizing Him as Sovereign over every area of our life. When we respect Jesus Christ as Lord of all, we will gladly surrender our all unto Him. That is true, biblical worship.**

In 1 Corinthians 3:21, the Apostle Paul said *"Let no man glory in men."* In 2 Corinthians 10:17, Paul said *"But he that glorieth, let him glory in the Lord."* In Galatians 6:14, he said *"But God forbid that I should glory, save in the cross of our Lord Jesus Christ, by whom the world is crucified unto me, and I unto the world."* **In a true worship experience, the music should never be exalted above the proclamation of the Word of God. But neither should the preacher be exalted above the message he has been sent to proclaim.** All of those who are privileged to lead others into worship should be very careful to see that nothing is exalted above Jesus Christ, to whom all the honor, all the praise, and all the glory belongs, forever and forever. *To Him be the glory in the church and in Christ Jesus to all generations."* (Ephesians 3:21 NASB)

Music is still very much a part of our worship experience today, although it is getting increasingly more difficult to find true worship music in the church. **Sadly, the envelope of church music has been pushed too far, too quickly, and it has brought disharmony and disunity to the fellowship, rather than true worship.** I think every church leader agrees something has to be done or else the church is going to lose either those who want more contemporary music, or those who want more traditional music, because the blending of the two isn't bringing harmony among the people. We all must earnestly pray that this wonderful, God-given medium will once again be used to glorify Him instead of man.

God also desires us to worship Him in truth! God not only deserves our worship, He demands it. But we dare not come before God on our own terms, or with our own agenda as to how we are going to worship Him, and with our concepts of worship. Our worship must be in the name of the One who has made us acceptable in God's sight, even Jesus Christ, His Son and our Savior, and it MUST be according to His will and His way, i.e., it must be according to the standards He has set forth in His Word. When we come before God, in the name of Jesus Christ, recognizing Him as our sovereign Creator, Sustainer, Redeemer and Lord, and renewing our submission unto His Lordship over our lives, then we can say we have truly worshiped God in truth.

In his book, *Strange Fire, Confessions of a false prophet*, Fred L. Volz said he had some wonderful experiences in his journey through the Charismatic movement. He said he received visions, told complete strangers about their past, and held sessions where he "decapitated Satan" through spiritual warfare. **He said, every experience was real, but they weren't true, meaning, true to Holy Scripture.** In the introduction of the book, Volz writes, *"It's time to prepare for a serious battle against that which seeks to lift imaginations, and every high thing that exalts itself against the knowledge of God."* (*Strange Fire, Confessions of a False Prophet*, TRION Press, 2003) While Mr. Volz's book is somewhat anecdotal, in that it is a testimony of his own experience, there is sufficient, observable confirmation to validate many of his assertions. For in many churches today, books about God have replaced the preaching and teaching of the true Word of God, especially in what he terms the "Word-Faith" movement.

Over the past few years, the *Purpose Driven Life,* by Rick Warren, has also captured the minds of people of all denominations. Pastors and leaders abandoned their normal schedules for what he termed the "forty days of purpose." a time for each person to find the true purpose for which God created them and gifted them, and how they can find true fulfillment in their Christian life, if they will focus on that one purpose.

I am confident that the study of this book motivated some to a deeper study of God's Word, but **when a book about the Bible, regardless of its content, or intent, replaces the Book of the Bible in our preaching and teaching, we have ceased to worship God in truth**. When what a man says about God's Word is exalted above what God's Word says about Himself, the heart-focus has shifted, and the true worship of God has been replaced by the ideas, concepts, and vain philosophies of man. Certainly, Jesus had this in mind when He scolded the scribes and Pharisees: *"Ye hypocrites, well did Isaiah prophesy of you, saying, this people draweth nigh unto me with their mouth, and honoreth me with their lips; but their heart is far from me. But in vain they do worship me, TEACHING FOR DOCTRINES THE COMMANDMENTS OF MEN."* (Matthew 15:7-9, Emphasis mine)

The Old English word for worship (*weordhscipe*) was translated into our English word, "worthship," meaning **to give honor to someone worthy of such recognition**. The biblical use of the word includes, as we previously stated, the act of prostrating oneself before the one who is worthy to receive such an honor, and "to kiss" their ring, or their hand, or even their feet.

God alone is worthy to receive all the glory and all the praise we could give unto Him, in return for what He has given to us, through Jesus Christ. **True worship then is a time of reflection and reverence for what God has done for us through Jesus Christ**. To focus on anything, or anyone else, regardless of the subject, or the amount of interest, or even the value of the truths or principles being taught, is to shift the focus from God's desire and demand for us to worship Him, to our need for answers to life's circumstances and problems. God becomes a benevolent benefactor whom we try to use as a means to help us achieve our own selfish and self-centered goals of self-fulfillment. In other words, the motivation for our being in worship becomes something for our own benefit, rather than a time, set aside, sanctified as "The Lord's Day," a day to honor Him and glorify Him for Who He is and for what He has already done.

Therefore, it is not that important that we get anything out of worship, because true worship is not about us! True worship is about Him! What is important is that we come before a Holy God, in the name of the One who has made that entrance possible by the shedding of His own precious blood, and we GIVE HIM the glory and the honor and the praise that is due His holy name. **Anything less is religion – man's feeble attempt to appease God with his good works, self-righteousness and religious activity.**

This appeal for more relevance in preaching is, as Michael Horton put it *"the call of the old Adam for more self-help. Think of the substitutes we have devised for the ordinary preaching of the law in our day: Every gimmick, slogan, or event that can possibly shift the focus from the sinner's peril to some behavioral change...when the very thing a seeker needs is to be brought to the end of his or her rope with no way of escape but Christ and His righteousness."(A Better Way,* Baker Books, a division of Baker Publishing Group, 2002)

What is needed in our preaching today is not more relevance, but more revelation. Preaching Jesus Christ and Him crucified is more than good advice or good ideas; it is the proclamation of the good news of what God has already done for us, by His amazing grace, and for which we should be thankful, rather than as a motivation to get the hearers to do something that is not within their power to do, or even with God's help can do.

Preaching is what God has said about Himself, His love for us, and how He has expressed that love through the gift of His only begotten Son, who became our Savior, and this is the central issue in true, biblical worship.

In the book, *Give Praise to God,* R. Albert Mohler, Jr., President of Southern Baptist Theological Seminary, wrote

> *"Expository preaching is central, irreducible, and nonnegotiable to the Bible's mission of authentic worship that pleases God...the anemia of evangelical worship – all the music and energy aside- is directly attributed to the absence of genuine expository preaching. Such preaching would confront the congregation with nothing less than the living and active word of God. That confrontation will shape the congregation as the Holy Spirit accompanies the word, opens eyes, and applies that word to human hearts."* (*Give Praise to God,* Ryken, Thomas & Duncan, P&R Publishing Company, 2003)

In his book, *God has spoken,* as cited by Dr. Stephen F. Olford in the introduction to the purpose and program of the Institute for Expository Preaching, Dr. J.I. Packer wrote:

> *"At no time, perhaps, since the Reformation have Protestant Christians as a body been so unsure, tentative and confused as to what they should believe and do. Certainty about the great issues of the Christ faith and conduct is lacking all along the line. The outsider sees us staggering from gimmick to gimmick and stunt to stunt, like so many drunks in a fog, not knowing at all where we are or which way we should be going. Preaching is hazy; heads are*

muddled; hearts fret; doubts drain our strength; uncertainty paralyzes action. Why is this? We blame the external pressures of modern secularism, but this is like Eve blaming the serpent. The real trouble is not in our circumstances, but in ourselves. The truth is that we have grieved the Spirit and God has withheld the Spirit. We stand under divine judgment. For two generations our churches have suffered from a famine of hearing the words of the Lord. For us, too, the Word of God is in a real sense lost." (*God Has Spoken*, Intervarsity Press, 1979)

If Dr. Packer is correct, and I think the evidence is ever before us, **the majority of Christians have never been exposed to true, biblical, expositional preaching, and therefore, the reality is that neither have they experienced true, biblical worship!** That is why there seems to be no real hunger and thirst for true righteousness on the part of the modern believer; they have been, and are still being taught that God will accept them without it.

Having been in the ministry now for 30 years, and 13 of those as a Senior Pastor, and having spent hours and hours in the study, often on my face before God, pleading with Him to guide me to that next paragraph or that next point in the outline, and then listening to the comments from the people as they leave the church, I can well understand what Paul meant when he referred to preaching as "foolishness!" If you consider the amount of time, money and effort that has gone into preparing the preacher as well as in preparing the sermon, over against the length of time those who are going to hear it will remember it, from man's perspective, you can't help but call that foolishness. Surely, many are saying, there must be a better way to communicate the gospel message than preaching!

But preaching is where the power of God is released.

In Romans 1:6, the Apostle Paul said *"For I am not ashamed of the gospel, for it is the power of God for salvation to everyone who believes."* (NASB) In Romans 10:17, Paul said *"Faith cometh by hearing, and hearing by the Word of God."* (but) ...*"How then shall they call upon Him in whom they have not believed? And how shall they believe in Him whom they have not heard? And how shall they hear without a preacher?'* (Romans 10:14 NASB)

One would think that preachers today are ashamed of the gospel as they try to couch it in phrases and slogans designed to attract the attention of the "unchurched", or the "seekers" who have little or no understanding of theological terms. But, I admonish my fellow pastors to remember that **God has not only called us as His "messengers" (the preacher), but He has also given us our "message"** (the pure, unadulterated gospel), **and He has also ordained the "method" by which that message is to be delivered** – "by the foolishness of preaching!" The emphasis of our sermons is to be on God's revelation of Himself to man, and mans need to respond to that revelation, not whether the lost or saved agree with it, or even understand it; that is the work of the Holy Spirit. We should certainly stop trying to make God relevant to man, which is not only impossible, but very irreverent and bordering on heresy.

As I said in the introduction, pastors are being told and taught today that the old style proclamation of the Word of God will not work with today's generation of hearers; their attention span is too short or their lack of knowledge about spiritual things prevents them from understanding deep spiritual truths. But may I remind you of what Paul said in 1 Corinthians 1:25 *"The foolishness of God is wiser than men"* and that is certainly applicable in terms of the preaching of the Word of God.

We have been dumbing down doctrine and relaxing our standards of worship for more than 35 years now.

Has it worked? Is it working? Look at the results! There is less attendance in church today than there was 35 years ago. And even with all of today's modern technology, available media sources, Christian books, tapes, conferences, and etc., the average church member knows less about the Bible and even less about real theology and God's plan for our redemption than most of our forefathers did with only a single copy of a King James Bible to read. The truth is, all we have done is trivialize truth, casualized Christ and weakened our witness to the world. **The lost world doesn't disrespect us because of our convictions, but because of the lack of them.**

In a seminar recently, the leader reported the latest findings from a survey regarding the attitudes of the unchurched toward the church. He told the group, some of whom were young preachers, that if they wanted to reach the lost and the unchurched in their communities they must lower the barriers that hinder them from coming to their church. He proceeded to mention some things like traditions, the style of music, the dress codes, including the preachers, how the preacher preached and the content of his sermons. He concluded with a warning that *"While we may look at them as good things, if they hinder someone from coming to Jesus, then we will have to answer for it!"*

After I took a walk to get my blood pressure down, I began to think about what he had said in context with some other areas of life, and I began to laugh. If we applied that same logic to some other circumstances of life, the conclusions would be illogical. And then I thought of these quite silly examples, again, just to release some pent-up pressure!

Suppose a man is bleeding profusely, and unless he gets medical attention quickly, he will probably die. Would he tell the ambulance driver not to stop at a Baptist hospital because he didn't like their traditions? Suppose a man is drowning in the ocean. Would he not cry out for help because the people on the shore were wearing coats and ties? Would a broken-hearted man not receive the wise counsel from a man just because he had to go to a church building, fill out some forms and be asked a few personal questions?

Suppose it had been days since I had eaten and I was very hungry. But when I entered the restaurant I told the manager, *"Sir, I was ready to eat in your restaurant, but you have some barriers that are keeping me away. And if I starve to death, it's going to be your fault!"* So, he asks me, *"What are the barriers that hinder you from eating with us?"* And I tell him, *"Well, sir, it's your building! I would prefer that it did not look like a restaurant. It's your music! I really don't want to hear that twangy, twang, twang! It's the dress code of your staff; those skirts are too long and the cook's hair is too short! It's the kind of food you serve; I'm just not accustomed to that. And, by the way, your menu is hard to read, I just can't find what I'm looking for!"* Finally the man says to me, *"Sir, maybe you aren't really as hungry as you thought you were!"*

When the Holy Spirit is drawing a lost person to Jesus Christ to be saved, even the powers of hell itself cannot keep him away. How is the pulpit a barrier to a person who wants to hear the true gospel of Jesus Christ? How is the Lord's Supper Table a barrier to a person who wants to receive the everlasting benefits of the Lord's death? How is the singing the great hymns of our faith a barrier to someone who says they want to know the wondrous story of God's amazing grace and boundless love?

Someone said to me several years ago, *"Wayne, it is the 'age of the Spirit and things must be different in the church if we are going to* reach today's generation." I said to him *"Friend, I am all for allowing the Holy Spirit absolute freedom in our worship services, but what I am seeing in the church today is not the activity of the Holy Spirit, (Acts 2:42) but actions that reflect the "spirit of the age" we are living in, (2 Thessalonians 2:3-12) and the Holy Spirit is grieved by it."*

Let's be honest, **there are no human hindrances to keep lost people from coming to a true, biblical worship service, if the Holy Spirit draws them**. And, the only barrier to a person accepting Jesus Christ as their Savior and Lord is their own unbelief. These so called "barriers" are our beliefs, our values, and our convictions; distinctives that set us apart from the world. The church is supposed to be different from an office building or a shopping mall. Perhaps to some, wearing their best to the worship service represents their attitude toward God. If they had an appointment with the President of the United States, they certainly would not greet him in golf shorts, so why would they dress any less for the King of Kings and the Lord of Lords? And besides, **if the church must do all of the adjusting in order for the lost world to come to Christ, then all you have is a church filled with lost people, who perhaps erroneously think they are saved by being there.**

Part Two: God's Design for Worship

So, what is the answer to this need for a true, biblical definition of worship? The writer of Hebrews said it so clearly. *"Wherefore we receiving a kingdom which cannot be moved, let us have grace whereby we may serve God acceptably with reverence and godly fear: For our God is a consuming fire."* (Hebrews 12:28-29) **If we are going to truly worship God, we must come before Him *"acceptably"* on His terms, not ours, and according to His Holy Word, not according to the books of man.** And we must come before Him with *"reverence and godly fear!"*

The contemporary church has lost its reverence for the holiness of God. In his book, *Truth Matters,* Pastor John MacArthur writes*: "True worship demands the sense of holiness, the sense of my sinfulness and the cry for purging. That's the essence of the proper attitude of worship."* (*Truth Matters*, Thomas Nelson Publishers, 2004) What a contrast to the flippant attitude expressed by many worshipers today.

In Romans 12:1, the Apostle Paul said *"I beseech you therefore, brethren, by the mercies of God, that ye present your bodies a living sacrifice, holy, acceptable unto God, which is your reasonable service."* In Psalm 15:24, David asked *"Who shall ascend into the hill of the Lord? Or who shall stand in his holy place? He that hath clean hands, and a pure heart; who hath not lifted up his soul unto vanity, nor sworn deceitfully."* The writer of Proverbs said *"The fear of the Lord is the beginning of wisdom."* (1:7)

I'm not sure many of today's pastors and leaders really want a true, biblical definition of worship, because it is so contrary to what they are doing in their churches to draw the crowds. But in their desire not to offend their attenders, or to lose some of their members, they have snubbed a holy God and lost His power, His blessing, and His glory! But, **when the glory of the Lord departs from a church, it may**

continue to have meetings and the crowds may continue to grow, but there is no way they can experience true worship.

If we really expected to meet a holy God in our church next Sunday, I don't think we would approach Him with the haughtiness and pride, or with the giddiness and glee that we see expressed in many of those who attend worship services today. I think we would bow before Him, repentantly, and give Him the glory, honor, praise and recognition that He rightly deserves. I believe we would fall on our knees and truly worship Him!

In his book *A Better Way,* Michael Horton says, *"the focus of worship these days seems to be on what we are doing, how we are feeling, and how we intend to respond...and we are caught up in our own 'worship experience', rather than in the God whose character and acts are the only proper focus." (A Better Way,* Baker Books, a division of Baker Publishing Group, 2002*)*

Today, the "style" of worship has become both the object and the subject of our worship, and therefore what is "done" as acts of worship have become the measure of our worship. **But in true, biblical worship, God is not only the object of our worship; He must also be the subject of our worship.**

In his commentary on the Psalms, as cited by Michael Horton in *A Better Way,* John Calvin used the analogy of a theatre to describe the real purpose of a worship service. Calvin said:

> *"The Church is a distinguished theatre on which the divine glory is displayed."* (Ps. III: 194); *"The Church, which God has selected as the great theatre where his fatherly care may be manifested."* (Ps. III; 12); *"The state or kingdom of the Church constitutes the principal and august theatre where God presents*

and displays the tokens of his wonderful power, wisdom, and righteousness." (Ps. IV: 335); *"The whole world is a theatre for the display of goodness, wisdom, justice, and power, but the Church is the orchestra...the most conspicuous part of it."* (Ps. V: 178). *(A Better Way,* Baker Books, a division of Baker Publishing Group, 2002*)*

In Calvin's day, and for hundreds of years afterwards, even the structure of the church building was a symbol to the community; a visible sign of man's need for God, and God's desire to meet with man. These massive buildings were often the most expensive and ornate buildings in the city, and when people entered their doors, there was an awesome sense that this place had been built and set apart for something unique, something special, something other than what was going on in the world. In many of these buildings, everything pointed upward, the rafters in the ceiling, the tops of the stained-glass windows, and even the tops of the ends of the pews. The furniture was mammoth and elaborate; again, visibly different from the furniture used in a home or a place of business. The pulpit was high above the congregation, with the Lord's Supper table beneath it, and the baptismal pool being very conspicuous.

Truthfully, we know that **God does not inhabit anything that was made by man; man himself is the temple of the Holy Spirit.** But practically, a statement was being made to those who entered those church buildings that those bricks, those boards, those windows, those doors, those pews, those walls, those rafters and that roof of that house had been built and set aside for one purpose and one purpose alone: to worship God! It wasn't the materials they used, or how they were structured. It was the motive and intent of their heart. **They wanted their building to point people toward God!**

Contrast that with **today's "worship centers" which are designed more like a theatre for the display of the glory of man, rather than as a "sanctuary" set apart as a place for man to worship God and to give Him the glory He deserves.** Some have even removed the pulpit, the sacred desk that separated, at least symbolically, the messenger from the message. By standing behind the pulpit, the preacher was making a statement that he was not there to deliver his own message, but a word from the Lord. Now, preachers are being taught that they need to come out from behind the pulpit, so as to remove that "barrier" between them and their audience. In other words, they are being taught to identify with the people more than with their position as the preacher.

When former President Jimmy Carter donned a pair of blue jeans and walked down Pennsylvania Avenue, and into the White House, he was making a statement that he was the people's President. His heart motive was pure. He was a peanut farmer from Georgia, who had just been elected President of the United States, and he wanted to be cordial and inviting to everyone. In retrospect, what President Carter did was to focus the attention of the people upon him as a man, rather than upon the highest office in the land, if not the whole world, the Office of the Presidency. As a result, he forfeited his position of respect. Some historians have said he never regained the respect of the people as the President, and to large degree, that lack of respect tainted his abilities and strengths to deal with some of the foreign policy issues that plagued his presidency, even up to the very last day.

I think the same principle can be applied to those of us who are called to preach today. If we do anything to draw attention to ourselves, rather than to Jesus Christ, we are stepping into the spotlight of glory that rightfully belongs to Him and to Him alone. If we do anything in order to help us identify with the people, rather than to model before them what it means to be "in Christ" and "Christ in me" then we may give up the respect that rightfully belongs to the office of the pastor. With so many pastors and ministers resigning every week, and some of them being outright fired for various causes and offenses, it is obvious that the office of Pastor/Teacher no longer enjoys the respect among the people that God intended, and still desires it to have.

Perhaps we need to heed the admonition of the Apostle Paul when he told the people at Corinth who were bragging about their favorite preacher *"let no one boast in men. For all things (pertaining to Christ) belong to you, whether Paul or Apollos or Cephas, or the word or life or death or things present or things to come; all belong to you, and you belong to Christ, and Christ belongs to God!"* (1 Corinthians 3:21-23 NASB) Paul said the message did not originate with man, belong to a man or rest in the wisdom of men. It was a message from God to be delivered by men to men; it belonged to the people.

Then in Chapter 4:1-2, Paul turned his attention to those men whom the people were arguing over as to which one was the best preacher, and he said *"Let a man regard us in this manner, as servants of Christ and stewards of the mysteries of God. In this case, moreover, it is required of stewards that they be found faithful."* (NASB) The word "servant" in this verse means more than a house maid or a butler, it was used to describe an under-rower, a slave, often chained to his bench, and forced to work the mighty oars that moved the mighty ships. They could not give up, give out or give in until the ship had reached its destination.

That isn't quite the glamorous portrait most pastors have of themselves, or how they would like their congregation to view them. And that word, "steward" means to be placed in charge of something that doesn't belong to us. **Simply stated, pastors are messengers, sent by God, to God's**

people, with a message from God's word. It isn't about us, and it isn't our message. We have no authority to adapt, change or in anyway alter the message. We have been sent by God to preach the word, to proclaim the message God has burned into our hearts with our lips and our lives, and to give up our lives, if necessary to get the message through to those He instructs us to give it to!

In 1 Chronicles 16:23-36, King David gave us the biblical definition of worship. First, in verses 12-21, David told the people to *"Remember his (God's) marvelous works that he hath done, and the judgments of his (God's) mouth."* **So, the first element in true, biblical worship is to remember the works of God.**

The Levites led the people in reciting what they called the Psalm of deliverance, referring to that time when God delivered the Hebrews from their slavery in Egypt, and how the entire Egyptian army drowned in the Red Sea, by the hand of God. The judgments of His mouth refer to the words of doom God gave to Pharaoh for not letting God's people go when Moses first asked him to. This one event was forever etched on the heart of every Hebrew, and it is still recited today at almost every Jewish festival.

When we were saved, God delivered us from our slavery to sin, and set us free from the power of sin through the death and resurrection of Jesus Christ. And when we have our own personal quiet times with the Lord, or when we gather together as the family of faith for corporate worship, the first thing we ought to do is to remember His marvelous work of redemption in us, and to glorify His Holy Name.

I know it is ancient, but I still love to sing that little chorus, *"Thank You, Lord, for saving my soul. Thank You, Lord, for making me whole. Thank You, Lord, for giving to me, Thy great salvation, so rich, and free!"* This was a "praise chorus" in my day, but it communicated a doctrinal truth to me that I have never forgotten. I also like to sing the third stanza of *"It Is Well With My Soul!"* My sin, Oh the bliss of this glorious thought! My sin, not in part, but the whole; Is nailed to that cross, and I bear it no more, Praise the Lord, Praise the Lord, O my soul!

David instructed his people to remember their deliverance from slavery, as we are to remember our own deliverance from sin. **But in verse 13, David also told them to remember who they were as the people of God.** *"O Ye seed of Israel, his servant, ye children of Jacob, his chosen ones."* God Himself chose Israel to be a people for Himself; a special treasure above all the people of the earth; the very apple of His eye.

Peter said we are a *"Chosen generation, a royal priesthood, an holy nation, a peculiar people; that ye should shew forth the praises of him who hath called you out of darkness into his marvelous light."* (1 Peter 2:9) Sometimes, in the midst of the battle, we tend to forget who we are in Christ. As we compare our particular circumstances with those in the world, we are often tempted to slip into the pit of envy, as we perceive their lives to be filled with pleasure and ease.

In Psalm 73, the Psalmist admitted that he had the same feelings as he compared his life of frustration and challenge with the prosperity of the wicked and their unconcern for their eternal future. In verses 13-14, he even thought he had cleansed his heart in vain and given up some worldly pleasures for nothing. But in verse 17 he said he had a change of heart *"Until I went into the sanctuary of God; then understood I their end."*

That's true worship! We don't need to hear sermons and messages on all that is going wrong in the world, we already know that, and if we don't, such information is readily available from a variety of sources. What is needed are sermons that remind us of who we are in Christ, and how we can live in this world without succumbing to its pressures and temptations. And as we review how God preserved the people of

Israel through one heartache and calamity after the other, especially in the reading of the Psalms, we can draw the conclusion that God loves those He has called His own, and His heart is always love toward them, even in those times of discipline. Those words can encourage us to keep on keeping on, even when we "feel" like we are walking alone.

I have a saying I repeat to myself when I get to feeling low and worthless. I urge you to copy it down and repeat it to yourself every day until you not only believe it, but you begin to rejoice in it:

> I was a sinner on my way to hell, when God, in His love and His great mercy, reached down and saved me by His marvelous, matchless grace. He redeemed me through the shed blood of Jesus Christ, adopted me as His child, and made me an heir to a mansion in His kingdom in heaven. I have been bought with a price, sanctified and set apart for His use. Therefore I no longer belong to myself. My body is now the temple of the Holy Spirit, the very dwelling place of God. I am to walk in this world as if I no longer live, but that Christ is actually living His life through me.
>
> This life is but a few years that pass away, like a vapor. I know that I am never more than one heartbeat away from the death of this life. So, I must make sure I seize every moment of each day for Christ, and invest them in the things that will bring Him glory, honor and praise. I am promised a new life on the other side of death; a life of everlasting fellowship with God, and with the family of God. I am indebted to Him for all that I am, and all that I will ever be. And the greatest joy of my heart is to know that nothing can ever change what God has already done in my life, through Christ Jesus.

Therefore, I am resolved to live this day as a dedicated, determined and devoted disciple of Christ. I know that I can do nothing of value without Jesus doing it through me. But I also know I can do all the things Christ will empower and enable me to do, for His glory.

In verse 15, **David said they were to remember the covenant God had made with them, through Abraham**. That covenant, which was confirmed through Isaac and Jacob (vs 16) was God's Word that He would never forsake them nor neglect to keep His promises to them. In verses 18-21, David outlined how God had kept that covenant by not allowing anyone to oppress them, and by warning the kings not to touch God's anointed, or to do harm to His prophets.

We, too, live under a covenant with God, which was secured for us through the death, resurrection and ascension of Jesus Christ. Through the death of Jesus Christ, we have the covenant of our redemption, the forgiveness of sin. Through the resurrection of Jesus Christ, we have the covenant of everlasting life. Through the ascension of Jesus Christ back into heaven, we have the covenant of our eternal home in heaven, and nothing can every separate us from that covenant, because it is sealed by our Savior's blood.

So when we gather in our places of worship, we, too have much to remember. We remember how he delivered us from sin. We remember who we are in Christ. We remember God's promise that He will never leave us nor forsake us, but that He will come again very soon, to take us to be with Him forever. And for that promise alone, He is worthy of our worship, our thanksgiving and our praise, which brings us to the second element in true, biblical worship.

Not only are we to remember His works, but, according to verses 23-26, we are to return His glory to Him. The only adequate response to God's mighty work on our behalf is to return unto Him the glory and honor He rightly deserves. We do that through our worship of Him with music, the reading of His Word, the observance of the Lord's Supper, baptism, prayer, preaching and the fellowship of the saints, the very outline of the activities of the New Testament Church as given in Acts 2:47ff. Everything we do in our worship service, from the time we enter the door of the sanctuary until the time we leave should be focused upon the Lord, and how we have gathered there to return unto Him the glory, honor and praise He so rightly deserves.

In verse 23, David admonished them to *"Sing UNTO THE LORD, all the earth"* (Emphasis mine). This is why the music we select for corporate worship is so significantly important. The words matter, the melody matters, the arrangement matters; all of it matters, because the music should be designed and presented for the praise and worship of Almighty God, not for the entertainment or even the benefit of those in the service. Music becomes a tool, through which we can offer praise unto God for what He has done for us, through Jesus Christ. It is supposed to be different from the music of the world.

Perhaps the best known Christian song of the last century was, "How Great Thou Art!" After remembering all the worlds the hand of God had made, and how, throughout the universe, God's power was displayed, the writer brought it down to his own heart, and said, *"And, when I think that God, His Son, not sparing, sent Him to die, I scarce can take it in. That on the cross, my burden gladly bearing, He bled and died to take away my sin."* Then, he returns the glory to God with that wonderful chorus, *"Then sings my soul, my Savior, God, to Thee! How Great Thou Art! How Great Thou Art!* "Amen and Amen!

The greatest hymnbook in the world is the Book of Psalms; 150 anthems, hymns and choruses, each with their own melody, meter and rhythm. No, we don't have to limit our worship music to those psalms, but I do believe we would be blessed to use them as a standard for the kind of music that God desires be used to truly worship Him.

But David said we are not only to return unto the Lord our worship, but we are also to return our witness. In verse 24 he says, *"Declare his glory among the heathen; his marvelous works among the nations. For great is the Lord and greatly to be praised!"*

The word "declare" means to proclaim or to preach. It means to tell others of our great salvation through Jesus Christ. We are living witnesses among the heathen of God's great power to save. We are examples on display of what God's amazing grace can do with one sinner who truly believes, and receives God's gift of salvation. In verse 25-26, the writer said God: *"is to be feared above all gods; for all the gods of the people are idols."*

Certainly, this must be done in good taste and in good order, as the Apostle Paul said in 1 Corinthians 14, but there needs to be a testimony time in every service, perhaps at the end, where folks can tell each other of the great things God has done for them, and is doing for them. We need to let each other know that the main reason we are in the sanctuary each Sunday is to tell the world that Jesus Christ is Lord of our lives, and we want to give Him the glory, and the honor and the praise for all He has done, and all He continues to do for us. This kind of testimony will prick the hearts of those who are not saved, and spur their interest in wanting to know more about Jesus. They might intellectually argue with the preacher about what the Bible says, but they can't argue with a changed life.

In verses 28 and 29, the writer gave us another way to express our witness, and that is through giving. Some translations use the word "ascribe" but the original Hebrew word means "to give!" *"Give unto the Lord, ye kindreds of the people. Give unto the Lord the glory due His name; bring an offering, and come before Him, worship the Lord in the beauty of holiness."*

When we truly see God in all of His majesty, all of His beauty and all of His power, we will have no hesitation or reservation about giving Him the glory due His holy name. When we finally see God as our Creator, our Provider, our Sustainer and our Protector, we will have no problem giving Him the glory due His holy name. And the evidence that we truly recognize Him for who He is will be reflected in the offering we bring to give to Him, for the offering we bring is a reflection of our true heart toward God. Therefore, a part of every corporate worship service should be a time to return unto the Lord, a portion of that which He has blessed us with, as the evidence that we recognize that He is the owner of it all.

What was it that Cain would not do that caused him to have such anger in his heart that he actually killed his own brother? The Bible says he would not honor God with a proper offering as God had required. Cain brought an offering, but it was from the leftovers and not the "firstfruits" as Able had given unto God.

The word "offering" means more than giving cash money or writing a check as a tithe. Verse 28 says we are to *"give unto the Lord GLORY AND STRENGTH!"* (Emphasis mine) And, the last line of verse 29 says, *"worship the Lord in the beauty of HOLINESS."* (Emphasis mine) God doesn't want our money, He wants us. He wants us to come before Him personally, and express our thanks for His many blessings. The songwriter asked: *"What gift can we bring to the richest of Kings, who walked on the gold streets of glory? Our lives we can give, each day that we live, and we'll be like wise men, adoring Him!"* That is worship!

Perhaps just placing that offering envelope into the plate may be too impersonal for true worship! Perhaps that very act becomes like a payment to the church, or a percentage of commission on the money we made that week. Perhaps we need to allow the people to bring their offering to the front of the church, and pray before they give their offering. Then, if God reminds them of those whom they have offended, they can get their hearts right with God, go and be reconciled with their offended brother or sister, and then come, in "holiness" before the Lord, and give Him an offering that is worthy of His holy name.

A missionary reported that after he had been working in one small village for several years, the people of the church had caught the vision of sharing their faith in Christ with the other villages in that region. They had also recognized that their new brothers and sisters in Christ back in America had given their money to send their beloved missionary to them to tell the good news, and they wanted to take up an offering to send missionaries to the other villages to do the same. The only problem was, they had no money; they had never seen money, because they had no place to spend it.

So the village leader placed a large basket at the front of the church where they gathered on the Lord's Day, and told the people to just bring what they could and place it in the basket, that perhaps God would see their hearts and make their offering useful for his glory. One by one, the people passed by the large basket, and placed their offering into it. Some gave pots or pans, earthenware pitchers, hewn-out bowls, hand-made tools, live chickens and other food items they had prepared for themselves.

The missionary said he noticed the last woman in line had her face covered and turned down as she approached the basket. When it came her time to give, she stopped, turned to the crowd and said, *"All I have to my name is this garment that I am wearing. And since I cannot give that alone, I must go with it."* And the missionary said that woman climbed into that basket herself. She was so thankful for what she had received from others, and for what God had given to her through Christ, she wanted others to know, not only of such a gift, but also of the Giver. So, she gave herself! That is true worship!

In a recent interview with a Pastor Search Committee, I asked if I could share my heart with them regarding true worship, and they agreed. I was working on this book at the time, and the thoughts were fresh in my mind, but I did not want to go into such detail as we have here. So I simply told them that I longed for the day, when people would enter into a sanctuary and respect that place as if it was holy ground; a place that was dedicated and consecrated as a place for believers to gather on the Lord's Day to worship Him.

I shared with them that it was my desire to see everything in the service, from the opening call to worship to the last benediction be focused on God, and God alone; that we would never cheapen that holy hour with the trivial matters that need to be said or settled at another time, and that we would never weaken the purpose of that hour by having to do things to attract the attention of man. Because one of the greatest concerns I have every Sunday as a pastor is, that someone would attend our services, go through the order of service, sing the songs, listen to the sermon, even give an offering, but leave an hour later without having truly worshipped the Lord. And while we may not be able to do anything to make sure that is going to happen to all who enter, at least, for God's sake, we should not be doing anything that is going to hinder it.

Much of modern worship is man-centered. It is designed to meet the needs of man and to attract the attention of man. **True worship is God centered and designed to exalt a Holy God.** The music, the message, the methods should all be carefully examined to make sure they lead the people to remember the things God has done, and is doing, and to remind them to return unto Him all the glory, all the honor and all the praise.

One of the saddest texts in the Bible is the second chapter of Jeremiah, where God chastens the people of Judah for their apostasy. In verse 13, God said, *"My people have committed two evils: They have forsaken Me, the fountain of living waters, to hew for themselves cisterns, broken cisterns, that can hold no water."* In verse 5, God said, *"They walked after emptiness and became empty."* And, perhaps the saddest of the saddest words are in verse 6, *"And they did not say, where is the Lord?"* (NASB) God's people had forsaken Him and turned to worship worthless idols. **But God said the thing that bothered Him most was that they did not even know He was missing!**

They had forgotten Who had brought them out of the land of Egypt, and led them through the wilderness; a land of deserts and pits; of drought and deep darkness, a land that no one had ever successfully survived to cross, and therefore, a land where no one dwelt. They had forgotten Who had brought them into that land called Canaan, to eat the fruit from the trees they had not planted, and to drink from the wells they had not dug.

God said He brought His people into the land of plenty, just as He had promised, but they had defiled His land by their apostasy and rebellion. Neither the priests, nor the prophets missed the Lord. They were going right on with their worthless worship, without even realizing that God was not present.

God forbid, that in our desires to attract lost man to our houses of worship, we do the very things that drive away the very One we are supposed to be worshiping! What a royal waste of time that would be, not only to those who are there to worship, but to a lost world who needs to see the power of God manifested in and through our lives.

The church, gathered for worship on the Lord's Day, is the most estimable witness we can give to a lost world that God is our God, and we worship Him in reverence,

righteousness and respect. But, if that outward manifestation of our inward devotion to God is to be an effective witness, then our worship must be according to God's Word, and therefore, in God's way.

The Westminster Confession of Faith says,

> "The acceptable way of worshiping the true God is instituted by Himself, and so limited by His own revealed will, that He may not be worshiped according to the imaginations and devices of men, or the suggestions of Satan, under any visible representation, or any other way not prescribed in holy Scripture." (21:1)

I believe it is time we put away the books about worship and return to the Book of Worship; God's Holy Word, which provides us with God's desires and God's direction for both the structure and the substance of true worship.

True worship is not a dynamic evangelistic meeting where souls are being saved, although that may be a result or an effect. True worship is not a hyper-emotional gathering with great fellowship and love being expressed among God's people, although that also may be a blessed outcome. **True worship is where God's people gather together to meet God, to review His works on their behalf, to thank Him for their own salvation, to renew their covenant, and to enjoy a little foretaste of that fellowship which will theirs forever in heaven, and to return unto Him all the glory that is due His holy name.**

In the book, *Give Praise to God; A Vision for Reforming Worship"*, the authors wrote bout the concern the late Dr. James Montgomery Boice had about the shift from God-centered to human-centered worship in the church today. He said, in the last years of his life, Dr. Boice believed that *"many (if not most) Christians had forgotten the meaning of true worship. In seeking to explain this unfortunate phenomenon, Dr. Boice observed the following connections between contemporary culture and the evangelical church: (1) Ours is a trivial age, and the church has been deeply affected by this pervasive triviality; (2) ours is a self-absorbed, human-centered age, and the church has become, sadly, even treasonably self-centered; and (3) our age is oblivious to God, and the church is barely better, to judge from it's so called worship services."* (James Montgomery Boice, The Gospel of John, vol. 1: The Coming of the Light: John 1-4 1985; repr. Grand Rapids: Baker, 1999)

Ryken continues,

"In Dr. Boice's view, the result of God's dramatic disappearance from Christian worship could only be a catastrophic loss of divine transcendence, not only in our worship, but in every aspect of human life – whenever in the church biblical authority has been lost, Christ has been displaced, the gospel has been distorted, or faith has been perverted, it has always been for one reason; our interests have displaced God's and we're doing his work in our way. The loss of God's centrality in the life of today's church is common and lamentable. It is this loss that allows us to transform worship into entertainment, gospel preaching into marketing, believing into technique, being good into feeling good about ourselves, and faithfulness into being successful. As a result, God, Christ and the Bible have come to mean too little to us and rest too inconsequentially upon us." (See Boice, *Whatever Happened to the Gospel of Grace?* 176-78) (Cited in *Give Praise to God,* Ryken, Thomas &

Duncan, P&R Publishing Company, 2003)

The reason our worldly culture has made more difference in the church than the church has made in the culture can only be explained by the lack of God's presence, and therefore, His power in our worship services. In Paul's second letter to Timothy, he said this would be one of the ways that we could know that we are living in the last days. In 2 Timothy 3:1-5, the Apostle wrote,

> *"This know also, that in the last days perilous times shall come. For men shall be lovers of their own selves, covetous, boasters, proud, blasphemers, disobedient to parents, unthankful, unholy, without natural affection, truce-breakers, false accusers, incontinent, fierce, despisers of those that are good, traitors, heady, highminded, lovers of pleasure more than lovers of God; HAVING A FORM OF GODLINESS, BUT DENYING THE POWER THEREOF; from such turn away."* (Emphasis mine)

Not only are 53,000 people leaving the church every week and not coming back, and many of those are seasoned saints who are simply fed up with worthless worship, God Himself has abandoned much of our worship, and the saddest thing is, the noise is so loud and the numbers are so great, that not even many pastors realize He is missing.

In the 1970's, the greatest debate among evangelicals was over the inerrancy and infallibility of the Bible: was the Bible God's divine word to man, or was it man's word to man about God? Here we are, thirty five years later in a debate over the definition of worship, and yet no one wants to take the time to look into God's word to see what God says about how He expects to be worshiped! **So I guess it**

didn't really matter who won that 70's debate after all! It doesn't matter if the Bible is true or not, if we aren't going to obey it.

But beloved, there is coming a day when Jesus Christ will examine, not only our works and our worship, but the motives of our heart. And there will be many who will come before the Lord and say, *"Lord, Lord, have we not prophesied in thy name? And in thy name have cast out devils? And in thy name done many wonderful works? And then will I profess unto them, I never knew you; depart from me, ye that WORK iniquity."* (Matthew 7:22-23) (Emphasis mine) They were truly worshipping, but their worship was not true to God's word. That same statement could be said about much, if not most of evangelical worship today. It is not according to God's Word, and therefore it is unacceptable to Him. In fact, were it not for His mercy, the very fires of heaven would come and destroy it all, because it is an offense to His holiness; it is a sacrilege without any reverence for God.

In the tenth chapter of Leviticus, Moses recorded what happened to two young men who showed their disrespect for God by just trying to "spice up" the worship service a little. The Bible says, *"Nadab and Abihu, the sons of Aaron, took their respective firepans, and after putting fire in them, placed incense on it and offered strange fire before the Lord, which the Lord had not commanded them. And fire came out from the presence of the Lord* (meaning the Ark of the Covenant) *and consumed them, and they died before the Lord. Then Moses said to Aaron, it is what the Lord spoke, saying, by those who come near Me I will be treated as holy. And before all the people I will be honored."* (Leviticus 10:1-3 NASB) **God made it clear that any disobedience to His commands was a distraction to His glory; and such activity would not be tolerated.**

True worship includes our desire to be absolutely obedient unto God. Anything less, regardless of how beautiful, how lovely, how wonderful or how good it may be, is irreverence at best and blasphemy at its worst. It is taking God's name in vain, because our hearts are not in it. **True worship is the giving of all we are and all we have as our expression of thanks to the One who has revealed to us His absolute glory through Jesus Christ our Lord.** (John 1:14) It is Moses falling on his face before God at the burning bush. It is Isaiah falling prostrate before God, recognizing his own inadequacy as compared to the holiness of God. **True worship is our expression of gratitude for God's willingness to take the initiative, not only in creating us, giving us life and designing us with a purpose, but in allowing us to know Him, in all of His glory, and then desiring that the likes of us would glorify Him with our lives as well as our lips.** That is true worship!

Fellow believers, we must raise the standard in our worship of God. In our desire to reach out and to attract lost people with the contemporary style and concept of worship, we are offering "strange fire" on the altar of God; incense that He has not prescribed, and therefore an activity that He cannot accept as worship, much less bless its use in our lives. And in so doing, we are failing to communicate to the lost world the absolute holiness of God, which is why they have little, if any respect for God today, as evidenced by their lifestyle and behavior. And unless that standard is raised very soon, I believe we will see the fire fall from heaven and consume our worthless, wasted worship.

In Acts 17:23-31, Paul told the Athenians on Mars' hill, they were worshiping God in ignorance. *"...and the times of this ignorance God winked at; but now commandeth all men everywhere to repent: Because he hath appointed a day, in the which he will judge the world in righteousness by that man who he hath ordained."* And one day, Jesus Himself will do just that, as He comes to rule and to reign as King of

Kings and Lord of Lords. His glory will fill the temple, and all the earth will be silent before Him. There will be no presentations, performances or processionals – the Lord, Jesus Christ will be in His Holy Temple, and every knee will bow and every tongue will confess that He is Lord of all.

CHAPTER SIX

The Raising Of the Standard In Our Respect for the Word of God

If you have shopped at a Christian book store recently, you have probably seen the many different kinds of Bibles being published today. There are children's Bibles with all their favorite stories highlighted. There are special Bibles for youth that point out the questions of life that are relative to their generation. There are couple's Bibles, men's Bibles, and women's Bibles with all the verses highlighted for their life situation. Then, there are many "Study Bibles" with the cross references marked and a brief commentary on each verse, directed, of course to the particular purpose of that study. Then you have the various translations, paraphrases, audios and videos, and now, CD's and DVD's that have the potential of opening up the history of the Word of God like never before.

Given my stated distaste for much of what is happening in the contemporary church, one might conclude that I would be opposed to this marketing of God's Holy Word. On the contrary, I am not opposed to any method that will help get the Word of God into the hands, and hopefully into the minds of the people. I believe some of these tools can be very helpful in today's media-driven society to inspire some to a deeper study of God's Word. I have many of the study Bibles in my own library and use them in my own personal study, as well as in the preparation of sermons.

One that I like was a gift from Dr. Ed Vallowe called *The Defender's Study Bible.* Throughout the Bible, the author has offered his own commentary on specific verses of scripture that give a defense for the basic doctrines of our faith. While I haven't searched the whole Bible, I have seen where this can be of great help in finding those scripture passages that give a solid foundation to what we believe and why we believe it.

My concern is, even with all of the study helps, the average church member knows less about the Bible and even less about real theology and God's plan for our redemption than most of our forefathers did with only a single copy of a King James Bible to read. For, unless these tools help us understand the real purpose of the Bible, then all we have done with our study systems, age-graded and topical-centered commentary and the like, is trivialized truth, casualized Christ and weakened our witness to the world.

Many believers today think the Bible is like an encyclopedia, offering God's answer to every dilemma of their lives. But the Bible is not a book about subjects or about topics. For example, the Bible is not a book about science, yet all the research of man has not turned up one contradiction of any scientific statement made in the Bible. The Bible is not a book about history, yet not one error has been discovered in its dating of historical events. Even our calendar is based upon that central event of our Lord's birth. The Bible is not a book about philosophy, yet I challenge anyone to find another book, written by 40 or more authors, over a period of 1500 years, in 3 different languages, (Hebrew, Aramaic, and Greek) that gives a more concise understanding of the development of mankind. The Bible was not written to address every heartache or to answer every problem or to cover ever circumstance that may occur in our lives. Yet, if you will read it from cover to cover, you will discover every feeling, every emotion; every life-situation anyone could ever encounter is either mentioned or illustrated.

Now, the Bible does answer some of man's deepest questions: questions every person asks if they ever begin to think for themselves, rather than just follow the crowd. Some of those questions include, "Who am I?" "Why am I here?" Or, "What is the real meaning and purpose to life?" No other book answers those questions with such absolute certainty as does the Bible.

The Bible is the guidebook of life for those who want to avoid the pitfalls and the snares the evil one has set before us in his attempts to distract us or to discredit us and to eventually destroy us. It is the instruction book of life for those who want to stand before God with honor and respect, and who want to hear those wonderful words coming from the lips of our loving Lord, *"Well done, thou good and faithful servant!"*

But even when all of those deeper questions of life have been answered, the Bible still has an even higher purpose. The Bible is more than an intellectual book to be accepted or rejected by the mind of man. The Bible is God's personal Word to the spirit of every man, regardless of language, culture, education or social status. The purpose of the Bible is to lead us to see the Lord, Jesus Christ, as our Savior, sent from the heart of God, because of His great love. Therefore, the overarching theme of the Bible is the salvation of lost man: how *"God so loved the world, that He gave His only begotten Son, that whosoever believeth in Him should not perish, but have everlasting life."* (John 3:16)

While the Bible may have many other functions in our lives, the major purpose is to make us *"wise unto salvation!"* (2 Timothy 3:15) From the first word of

Genesis to the last word in Revelation, the Bible reveals God's plan for the redemption of man, and shows us what and how to believe in order to be saved. That plan centered in the birth, the life, the death and the resurrection of Jesus Christ: God Himself, born in the flesh, so He could die in the flesh, yet never less than eternal God, so that His death would be sufficient for the sins of all men.

I think it was W.A. Criswell, the famous preacher of the First Baptist Church in Dallas, Texas, who coined the phrase that one could cut the Bible at any chapter and any verse on any page, and it would bleed the blood of Jesus Christ who died for our sins. The Old Testament points toward the coming of the Messiah, the Savior of the world, and the New Testament points to it as having happened just the way God had said it would, and the dramatic change that came over the whole world as a result of those events.

The Bible is God's story of His redeeming love for lost mankind. No one man or group of men could have fabricated such a love story as we read in the Bible, much less devised a plan such as this. The Bible is God's love letter to lost mankind. It was written by God, and it has been, and will continue to be preserved by God, to be taught and preached to all who will listen. And those who open their heart to believe it will become "wise unto salvation" because they will know and understand that God's "whosoever" included them.

According to 2 Peter 1:20-21, even though the Bible was written by different men at different times and in different languages, their pens, or quills as it were, were moved by the Holy Spirit to write the absolute, infallible and inerrant Word of God. This is what is known as "divine inspiration!" God so superintended the writings, that what was written is absolute truth, with no mixture of error in content or intent, information or application.

Down through the ages, evil men have tried to destroy the Bible, but none have succeeded. One of those was the infidel, Voltaire, who declared that in 100 years after his death, the Bible would cease to exist. But, in the sovereignty of God, exactly 100 years later the printing presses that had printed Voltaire's books were printing copies of the Bible. God's Word is absolutely indestructible, until the Living Word returns to this earth. As the Apostle Peter said, *"The grass withereth and the flower thereof falleth away: but the Word of the Lord endureth for ever. And this is the word which by the gospel is preached to you."* (1 Pt. 1:23-24)

So, if we are going to raise the standard of Jesus Christ in the world today, if we are going to raise the standard in our love for the Lord, our neighbor, our church, and in our worship, we must begin by raising the standard of our respect for the Word of God. As Christians, we say we are people of "The Book!" But do we practice what we say we are, or have we turned to sources other than the Bible to find the answers for our questions?

There are many different kinds of voices speaking in the world today. There are voices of conversation – talk shows are the most listened to programs on radio and the most watched on television. Regardless of the subject matter, whether it is morality, politics, entertainment, gossip, or the most horrible examples of the depravity of man, you can find it discussed and displayed on a talk show. There are voices of information – more than 37,000 newspapers, magazines, journals, periodicals being published in the United States alone. Add to that the proliferation of books, tapes, seminars, conventions, plus the age-graded institutions of learning, the greatly expanded television programming, and the information super highway – the internet, where any kind of information from any kind of source is available at the click of a mouse.

The prophet Daniel said that one of the signs of the last days would be that *"many shall run to and fro and knowledge shall increase."* (Daniel 12:4) With the events of human history doubling and tripling, and quadrupling at such a rapid pace, truly we can conclude that we are living in what many are calling an "information overload" – there is just no way to process all of the available information through our finite minds, much less retain it for very long. Plus, there is no "truth filter" through which all of this information must be sifted before it reaches our ears and tries to change our minds.

This is why it is so important that the voices of proclamation be heard above all of the other voices in the world. The true preaching of the Word of God is that standard of truth by which we can measure all the other voices we are exposed to every day. Martyn-Lloyd Jones, in his classic work *Preaching and Preachers,* wrote: *"The most urgent need in the Christian Church today is true preaching; and as it is the greatest and most urgent need in the church, it is obviously the greatest need in the world also."*

But, as Michael Horton says in the introduction to his book, *A Better Way:*

> *"preaching today has lost its nerve. And so has worship in general, along with its effects: missions, evangelism, and diaconal care...preaching itself* {has been turned} *into a form of entertainment and emotional expressiveness. Further, whereas the reading material of pastors, elders, church musicians, and informed laypeople used to be quite serious theology, today's bibliographies include, in ranking order, marketing studies of the unchurched, pop psychology, practical management guides by successful CEOs, and peculiar end-times novels."*
>
> *(A Better Way,* Baker Books, a division of Baker Publishing Group, 2002*)*

Today, preachers are being taught and told not to preach

the Word. We are being told that the modern ear is not capable of hearing the typical, traditional preaching; that we should not use terms like sin, judgment, and never warn them about an eternal hell; that today's people will not listen to an in-depth, doctrinal sermon, and that we should avoid speaking about moral absolutes or consequences of sin and to "go light" on the scriptural references, for most folks will not know how to use their Bibles, even if they bring them along, and even if they are the same translation.

But it is my position in this book **that if the people in the pew are too shallow to hear the Word of God, it is because the preachers in the pulpits have neglected to preach the Word of God to them**. Horton confirms this from an historical perspective:

> *"The medieval church had accumulated many innovations in both doctrine and worship, and the average layperson knew little about the Scriptures. Worship services introduced morality plays, stirring music to excite a sense of mystery and majesty, and relied on images, 'the books for the unlearned', as the saying went. The Heidelberg Catechism of the Reformed Churches thundered back, 'No, we should not try to be wiser than God. He wants His people instructed by the living PREACHING OF HIS WORD – not by idols that cannot even talk.' If the people were not up to speed in the biblical maturity, the answer was to get them up to speed, not to accommodate to a degenerating condition."* (Emphasis mine)
> *(A Better Way,* Baker Books, a division of Baker Publishing Group, 2002*)*

True preaching, in the power of the Holy Spirit, rules out such things as a "Sunday Morning Talk" or "A Conversation on Biblical Themes" or a "Visual Demonstration of the Love of God through Interpretive Drama!" The central issue in preaching, especially as it relates to the Sunday morning service, is the faithful proclamation of the gospel, the Word of God, so the truth of God's word can penetrate the mind and move the heart of the hearer to adjust their lives in accordance to what they have heard. And to do that, the preacher must dig deeply into the Scriptures, grammatically, historically and doctrinally. And then, by the power of the Holy Spirit, he is to so apply that truth to his own life, that when he stands to speak, it is actually the text of the Scripture speaking through him. As J.I. Packer once said, *"the preacher becomes the mouthpiece of the text!"*

Preaching is God's chosen method to get the message of God's plan for man's redemption into the heart of lost man. That great theologian-preacher-pastor-evangelist, Paul, wrote: *"For the preaching of the cross is to them that perish foolishness; but unto us which are being saved it is the power of God...for after that in the wisdom of God the world by (its) wisdom knew not God, it pleased God by the foolishness of preaching to save them that believe."* (1 Cor. 1:18, 21) Sadly, many pastors today have forsaken the foolishness of preaching and have gone to preaching foolishness!

I believe our nation is less than one generation away from total paganism. In my lifetime, we have moved from being, basically a Christian nation, at least in terms of moral values and virtues, to a post-Christian nation and now to a anti-Christian nation, where Christianity is no longer accepted or respected as the predominant religion. And, if we are to see any change in the future; by that I mean, if our children are to have any hope of knowing God at all, the church must rediscover its mission and its ministry to expose people to the truths of the Word of God. And, history teaches us, the primary way that is done is through the preaching of God's Holy Word.

There is no clearer admonition in Scripture regarding

this than those three haunting words the Apostle Paul gave to his young preacher-boy, Timothy, in 2 Timothy 4:1-5: *"Preach the Word!"* For Paul, being a preacher was not a way to win a popularity contest; **it was a solemn responsibility**, given to him by God, for which there would come a day of accountability. In verse 1 of that passage, Paul gave Timothy some of the most challenging words he had ever spoken. Timothy, *"I charge thee therefore before God, and the Lord Jesus Christ, who shall judge the quick and the dead at his appearing and his kingdom, preach the Word!"* Paul was reminding Timothy that, while a congregation of people might be listening to him as he preached, the most important audience would be God and Christ Jesus, before whom he also would have to stand, one day.

Why did Paul consider preaching the Word such a solemn responsibility? The answer is in 2 Timothy 2:16, as Paul said *"All Scripture is given by inspiration of God, and is profitable for doctrine, for reproof, for correction, for instruction in righteousness."* Very simply, "doctrine" tells the hearer how God desires him to live. "Reproof" shows the hearer where he has missed the mark, or sinned against God's desires and design. "Correction" shows the sinner how to be reconciled to God, through confession, repentance, forgiveness and restoration. And, "instruction" shows the forgiven how to avoid that same pitfall again. And, since all Scripture is divinely inspired – meaning it is truth with no mixture of error at any point, it must be preached as such, for both God and Christ are watching to see if what the preacher preaches is true to their Word. It is a solemn responsibility, and it is not to be taken lightly, as some are doing today.

The Greek elucidation of the prepositional phrase, *"in the presence of"* literally means, *"in the face of."* The preacher is to preach the Word, not looking at the faces of the people for their approval and acceptance, but in the face of God and Christ Jesus, who not only gave the preacher the message, but who is also the very message itself. For to some degree, **the truth about God rests in the hands of those who have agreed to serve God as His preachers.** As the Apostle Paul said in 1 Corinthians 4:1-2 *"Let a man so account of us, as of the ministers of Christ, and stewards of the mysteries of God. Moreover, it is required in stewards, that a man be found faithful."*

But not only is preaching a solemn responsibility, it is also a specific responsibility, as the preacher is to preach nothing more, or nothing less than the Word of God. He is not to preach his own ideas about the Word, just the Word! He is not to preach about the faith or any part of the faith, but the very body of doctrines that establish, support, strengthens, qualify, clarify, illustrate or demonstrate the faith. The true preacher is a messenger sent from God. He cannot choose his own message, or the authority to adapt the one he has been given. His only decision is whether or not he will proclaim it, and if he will not, he should step down and let others speak who will be faithful to their calling.

In the Epistle of Jude, the writer warned of the coming judgment upon false teachers, those *"ungodly men, {who were} turning the grace of our God into lasciviousness, and denying the only Lord God, and our Lord Jesus Christ."* (Jude 4) He said the purpose of his letter was to *"exhort you* (the elders of the church) *that ye should earnestly contend for the faith which was once delivered unto the saints."* (Jude 3)

The Apostle Paul gave a similar exhortation to the Church at Thessalonica. *"Therefore, brethren, stand fast, and hold the traditions which ye have been taught, whether by word, or our epistle."* (2 Thessalonians 2:15) Yet, today, it seems the contemporary church is willing to eliminate all of those traditions and embrace every new idea and wind of doctrine that comes along, without ever questioning whether it is acceptable unto God. Such utter nonsense is destroying the unity of God's people in every denomination.

Today, the Word of God is being watered down to make it more palatable to the people. We have paraphrased it, revised it, torn it apart and topicalized it to answer our questions about life and how we can be successful in it. **But the more we have diluted it from its original texts, the less it is being read, and the less it is being obeyed, and therefore the less it is being respected.** In fact, the Word of God has become so trivialized, even though it is still one of the world's best sellers, it has lost its respect among the books that have been written about it.

Jesus never sought to make the truth of God's word more palatable to His hearers. In fact, Jesus often hid the truth in parables, hoping that what He did share and illustrate would whet their appetite to want to know more. He wanted them to think! To reason! To analyze! To compare what He was saying with what the countless other voices were saying! He knew that their faith in Him had to be built on a solid foundation of truth, not on little trite, catchy phrases that attracted their attention and that were easy to accept.

Too often, preachers want to "bring the message down to their level" when our assignment is to be lifting the people up to God's level. (See Ephesians 4:11-14) Too often we want to preach and teach something that is relevant to the life needs of those in attendance, when we ought to be preaching and teaching them what they need in their lives, the truth of God's Word! Too many preachers and teachers are "editing" the gospel for the benefit of their hearers. They don't want to endure the ridicule and the persecution that might come from those who may be convicted by the truth of God's Word. They don't "reject" the whole Bible; they just "select" those passages that are the least offensive and "reject" those that might cause controversy. They stay with the acceptable themes of the love of God and the goodness of man. They might talk about the sin of man, but never the "sins" of man, for fear of offending those with different views and values. The death of Jesus Christ, if it is preached at all, is viewed as a model of total sacrifice, an example to be emulated by those who are dedicated to a worthy cause. The resurrection of Jesus Christ, if it is preached at all, is presented as that overcoming power of goodness that lives on after our physical death, and continues to influence the lives of others. That is not only false teaching; it borders on heresy!

The death and resurrection of Jesus Christ is without any meaning whatsoever apart from the total, sinful depravity of man, and God's sovereign plan for man's redemption, through the sacrifice of Jesus Christ upon that cross. And if a preacher is a true, God-called herald of the King, he will preach the whole counsel of the Word of God; nothing more, nothing less, nothing else. And if that cuts cross-grain with his hearers, and they react negatively to him or to his message, then he should welcome their response as the evidence that he has been preaching just like Jesus did, for so did they persecute Him.

As the Apostle Paul said in Ephesians 4:15, we are to *"speak the truth in love"* so that we may *"grow up into him in all things, which is the head, even Christ."*

In 2 Timothy 4:2, Paul gave Timothy some specific methods of preaching, as he admonished him to *"be instant, in season, out of season, reprove, rebuke, exhort with all longsuffering and doctrine."* Being instant, in season and out of season means to take a stand on the Word of God whether it is acceptable or not, or whether it is popular or not.

There are some times when the Word of God is easy to preach, and folks will listen intently; a time of birth, or death, a time of joy, or sorrow, a time of peace or war. In those extreme times the Word of God is easy to turn to, and its precepts are easier to accept and apply.

But there are some seasons when the Word of God is not easy to preach, and the folks won't listen; when freedom has led the people into licentiousness and the preacher must call for repentance, when things seem to be going well and life is full of pleasure, and the preacher must call upon the people for a personal sacrifice; when everyone is crying "peace, peace", and the preacher must warn them of the judgment to come.

But the true preacher of the Word will keep his sense of urgency and preach, whether it is convenient or inconvenient; whether it is welcomed or unwelcomed; whether it is favorable or unfavorable. He is not to give up any opportunity to preach the Word, but to be "instant" – always prayed up and prepared, always ready to go, ready to speak, ready to preach the whole counsel of the Word of God without hesitation or reservation.

To reprove means to stir a person's soul so they can see their sin and feel the conviction of the Holy Spirit that may lead them to confession and repentance. To rebuke means to give a warning to those who are walking contrary to the ways of God of the consequences of their behavior, unless they repent and return to Him. To exhort with all longsuffering and doctrine means to be ready to comfort those who do repent, and encourage them with the truth of God's Word regarding their sin and God's forgiveness.

The word "exhort" in the Greek language means to come alongside of those people whom God has placed under our charge, and to never give up, give out or give in, until those babes in Christ have taken their first step of genuine faith and are able to continue walking with the Lord in the light of His Word, and are growing in the grace and knowledge of God. A true, God-called preacher will not be content to just preach to the masses; impressing them with his eloquence and learning. But he will be willing to get involved in their "messes", and impress upon their hearts the indelible imprint of the love of God, even with his very life, if necessary.

Thirdly, Paul's charge to Timothy reminds us that **preaching is a serious responsibility**. In verses 3-4, Paul said *"For the time will come when they will not endure sound doctrine; but after their own lusts shall they heap to themselves teachers, having itching ears, and shall turn away their ears from the truth, and shall turn to fables."*

There is no doubt in my mind whatsoever that we are living in that day, and anyone who knows the difference between the truth of God's Word and the myths and fables of man would have to agree. There is a "falling away" from the true gospel, and many, many preachers are falling away as well; preaching what the people want to hear, so they can keep their jobs, rather than preaching what they have been called to preach, and trusting God with their care. The results of this trend has been, and continues to be devastating to the real effectiveness of the church, as seasoned saints leave the church because they aren't being fed the truth, and the babes in Christ never grow up because they never hear the truth, or see it exemplified in the lives of mature Christians.

We are seeing that "falling away" right before our very eyes, as preachers are changing the Word of God to fit the lifestyles of their members, rather than to challenge the members to change their lifestyle to fit the Word of God. And young people, even many young adults with children, are being attracted to those churches where their lifestyle is not only accepted by the people in the church, but proclaimed as being acceptable by the man in the pulpit.

Many preachers have stopped preaching the Word and have turned the sermon time into a "talk show" dialogue-style message. Casual dress has replaced the tie and jacket. The conversational voice has replaced "thus saith the Lord!" Compromising for expediency has replaced the absolutes of God's Word. **Many preachers today are delivering cute little "sermonettes for Christianettes" – with lots of**

warm fuzzies and feel-good remarks, rather than proclaiming the truth of God's Word in the power of the Holy Spirit. And it is no wonder, because that is what the people want to hear. This is the error of "felt-need" preaching, and it is drawing crowds that look like a revival, but it is really apostasy – they have fallen away from the true faith.

In many churches, the singing of the great hymns of our faith has been totally replaced by short choruses, which are repeated over and over again, working the people up into such an emotional state that the "speaker" then can move them to do almost anything.

Several years ago, in at least two locations, attenders at one of these events were seen walking on all-fours, and barking like a dog. Others would lie on their backs and laugh for hours. Others would go into a corner and regurgitate their sins into a spittoon, and all of this was supposed to be a visible manifestation of the Holy Spirit. The person who observed this event with his own eyes said, when the preacher stood to preach, not a soul opened their Bible, or even indicated that they had brought one. It was pure emotion. I'm convinced the experiences these folks were having were real. The only problem is they weren't true – not true to the Word of God, and therefore, not a true expression of the Holy Spirit. They had been duped by a false prophet! This is what Paul said would be the result of shallow preaching – the people would *"turn away their ears from the truth, and shall be turned to fables."* (vs 4)

Let's be honest about it! If some Christian entertainer was to appear at our church on Sunday, someone who would stir our hearts with humor, get us clapping our hands and patting our feet with a song, or move us to even more physical excitement with a certain repeated rhythm, most likely the place would be packed out, even if there was a fee at the door to get in. People who had not been in church in years would come if some famous celebrity was going to share his testimony or some gospel group was going to sing some of the "good old songs!"

People who have "itching ears" want to hear the Christian message; they just don't want to hear about CHRIST! They want to hear the gospel in a way that entertains, not convicts; that is called apostasy – the falling away from the true faith. Once they have rejected the Word of God as truth, they turn to fables and myths, and believe every experience that happens to them in life is some kind of "sign" from God, affirming their "freedom" in the faith, when, in actuality, those experiences are the devices of the devil rewarding them for their freedom from the faith.

In an interview with a Pastor Search Committee, one of the members said she believed God could speak to some people through music just as well as He could through the preaching of the Word of God. That is the problem – many folks have abandoned the truth, God's Holy Word, because it is too convicting, and they are searching for a "message" that affirms their version of what it means to be a Christian or to have faith in God. Once truth has been rejected, "faith" is a matter of opinion, experience, preference or style. Those who have fallen for this lie have formulated their own set of beliefs and doctrines, worship format, as well as their own concept of God, Christ, the Holy Spirit, as well as what it means to be saved. And, sadly, this is what is being offered in many "niche-market" churches today – a form of the gospel in their own style; their own lifestyle, their own vernacular, whether it is a "boomer, buster or bubba" church, but they have denied its power. That is why many seasoned saints are leaving the church in droves, they can't tolerate such disrespect for God, or for God's Word, and they are doing exactly what Paul said in 2 Timothy 3:5. They are simply and quietly turning away from them, retreating to their own homes and having their own services with friends.

In 2 Timothy 4:5, Paul told his young son-in-the-faith to do several things: *"Watch thou in all things, endure afflictions, do the work of an evangelist, MAKE FULL PROOF OF THY MINISTRY."* (Emphasis mine) In other words, to be true to his calling, even to the very end, regardless of what it might require of him. Some preachers start out great but fall flat at the end, having compromised their convictions and adjusted their faith to fit in with their hearers. Others lose the moral high ground through some lack of integrity or doctrinal inconsistency. But the true preacher of the Word of God will give all he has spiritually, mentally, emotionally and physically, yet, all the time, pleading for the anointing power of the Holy Spirit, knowing that apart from that power, he will flounder in his own weakness, and accomplish nothing of eternal value.

Paul said he was ready to receive that Crown of Righteousness that awaited him at that last day; having fought the good fight, having finished his course, having kept the faith – not altering it, adjusting it, or adapting it to fit in with the vain philosophies of his day. His hearts desire was to see Timothy stand there with him on that great day.

Preaching is a serious responsibility, for which there will be a day of accounting. Preaching is the most demanding work anyone can do, as well as the most rewarding. It is humbling, yet exhilarating to enter the pulpit knowing God is with you. It is also very frightening to be in that pulpit and sense that God is not with you, that you are on your own. Why would God do that? Only He knows for sure, but I would believe it would be to remind us not to presume upon His grace, or just assume, that because we are there, so is He. For only when we have truly studied to show ourselves approved, as workmen who need not to be ashamed, able to rightly divide the word of truth, is God so inclined to anoint our labor with His mighty power. Until that occurs, it's all in vain!

It has been said that true evangelism is sharing the gospel of Jesus, in the power of the Holy Spirit, and leaving the results to God. The same axiom could, and should be applied to true, biblical preaching. It is my prayer that God will raise up a new generation of preachers who fear nothing but God, hate nothing but sin, and who will go into the world with that fire in their mouths, and preach the Word!

Forty years ago, some very bold, courageous and deeply committed men stood their ground regarding the absolute inerrancy of Holy Scripture. They said the Bible was truth with no mixture of error in its content as well as its intent. For forty years these men withstood the caustic criticisms of those in the halls of higher learning who thought they knew better than these uneducated preachers who were so ignorant as to believe the Bible was literally true – that Mary was a virgin, that Jesus did feed 5000 men plus the women and children with the few loaves and fishes, that Lazarus did come forth from the grave after four days, and so did Jesus after three, just as the Bible says. Many of these men suffered severe public persecution, not only from those outside their own denomination, but from those within, who saw this battle for the Bible as being nothing but politics and a hunger for power. Some of their families suffered greatly because of the physical and emotional stress these men encountered.

Looking back upon those events today, one can only imagine where we would be along the pathway to apostasy had these men not stood firm in their commitment to the truth of God's Word. For what these men did to right the ship of their own denomination also had an affect upon every other evangelical denomination as well. They changed the course of Christian history, at least for awhile.

During the heat of the battle, hundreds if not thousands of preachers and laymen rose to applaud the courageous stand these men were taking, and gave them every support they could, not only through their voices in the convention halls, but also in their respective pulpits as well. But as the years have passed, and along with them some of those old "fundamental" preachers, some of those same pulpits have now grown strangely silent regarding the Bible and its absolute authority over our lives. For just as our western culture has rejected the notion of an absolute truth, so has the church, in many ways, rejected God's Word as the absolute authority for our faith as well as the way we live our lives. And now, even as Christians, we find ourselves part of an evangelical group that no longer holds a view of truth on which we can make our stand, even if we could find the men to make it. And again, I repeat, **perhaps the greatest sin of all is that there is no great outcry from God's people that someone please lift up the standard of God's truth once again!**

CHAPTER SEVEN

The Raising Of the Standard In Our Compassion for the Lost And In Our Preservation of the Saved

Recently, Lifeway Publishing Company conducted a survey of pastors and other church leaders, regarding the top ten issues facing the church today. It was no surprise to see evangelism, or the lack of it, and discipleship were among the top five. The post-modern culture we live in reeks of selfishness and self-centeredness, and the contemporary model of "church" today not only reflects it, but enhances it, especially in its lack of compassion for the lost, and in its inability to preserve those who are saved.

The Bible doesn't use the term "unsaved" to describe the condition of those without Christ Jesus as their Savior and Lord. It uses the word "lost!" When God expelled Adam and Eve from that beautiful Garden of Eden, He gave us a very vivid picture of what it means to be lost. Because of their sin against God, Adam and Eve lost their freedom to live in that garden paradise and they lost their ease of life. They lost their independence, their fellowship with God, their respect for each other, and ultimately they lost their lives.

From the very second they disobeyed God, Adam and Eve never knew a moment or real peace or pleasure, without the negative and destructive influences of sin haunting their every move. That sin nature was handed down to their children, and the first murder on earth was recorded, as Cain killed his brother Abel. That sin nature was handed down to their children, and to every generation that followed. That same sin nature is in every child that is born today. That sin nature is in our hearts as well, even those of us who have accepted Jesus Christ as our Savior, and therefore are "saved." As the Apostle Paul said in Romans 5:12, *"Wherefore, as by one man sin entered into the world, and death by sin; and so death passed upon all men, for that all have sinned."*

Today, the majority of the people in the world are still "lost!" Having never seen the signs of salvation along the road of life, or just deliberately avoiding them, they are lost in the wilderness of sin and incapable of finding their way to everlasting life without someone coming to their rescue and leading them back to the right path. That is the mission of the church, and therefore of every true believer – to get the message of the gospel to the whole world.

It is the deepest burden of my heart to see lost people saved. But there is an equal burden on my heart for the saved to be discipled until they become reproducing reproducers (2 Timothy 2:2). I believe that is what our Lord had in mind when He gave us what we call the Great Commission, as outlined in Matthew 28:18-20. As we walk through this world, we are to be making, marking and maturing disciples for Christ – *"teaching them to observe all things whatsoever I have commanded you."* (VS 20)

When we go to the doctor's office to find the source of our physical problems, the first thing the nurse does is to stick that thermometer into our mouths to see if our body temperature is within the normal range of 98.6 degrees. If a Christian came before the Lord to find out why he was having spiritual problems, I believe the first thing our Lord would do would be to probe into his heart to measure his devotion to Him as it is reflected in his passion for those who are lost. For as our physical health is revealed by the temperature of our bodies, our spiritual health is revealed in our passion to see lost people come to know Jesus as their Savior, and saved people sharing their faith with others.

In the ninth and tenth chapter of Romans, Paul expressed his heart's desire to see his kinsmen saved. In chapter 9:1, Paul said: *"I say the truth in Christ, I lie not, my conscience also bearing me witness in the Holy Ghost, that I have great heaviness and continual sorrow in my heart. For I wish that myself were accursed from Christ for my brethren, my kinsmen according to the flesh."* In the first verse of chapter 10, Paul repeated that his *"heart's desire and prayer to God for Israel is, that they might be saved."*

As you recall, it was in Romans chapter eight where the Apostle Paul described a man who was filled and empowered by the Holy Spirit. Then, in chapter nine, he says the key evidence of that filling and empowering is a sincere passion to see those we love come to know Jesus Christ as their Savior and Lord.

That truth is also affirmed in the second chapter of Acts, as the disciples were gathered in the Upper Room, and the Holy Spirit came upon them in a mighty way, and they began to share the gospel of Jesus Christ in the many languages of those who had come for the celebration of Pentecost. The first evidence of their being filled with the Holy Spirit was in their passion to share the gospel with those who were lost.

Yet, research shows that **only two percent of believers in American churches regularly share their faith in Christ with anyone** – not even as a testimony of their trust in the Lord. Does that mean only two percent of American believers are filled and empowered by the Holy Spirit? We can't say that for sure, but it gives explanation for the impotency of the American church, compared to the tremendous potency of the church in third-world nations today.

It grieves me to say this, but **most American Christians have lost their sense of a holy God**. They do not understand His attributes of love, power, wisdom, sovereignty and grace. Many will go for days, weeks, even months, and never see God's activity in their lives, or realize what they are missing from Him.

In 1998, George Barna reported, of the 100 million Americans who attend church on any given Sunday, at least 50% of them will not have the full assurance of their own salvation. In other words, they do not know, beyond a shadow of a doubt, that they will go to heaven when they die. So the answer to our lack of evangelism is clear! How can they share what they don't have in their own heart?

The same survey revealed that 95% of those who attend church on Sunday do not understand the person and work of the Holy Spirit. If only 5% of church attenders understand what it means to be filled and empowered with the Holy Spirit, then it is no wonder that only 2% of American believers ever share their faith in Christ with anyone, even with those they love. **And the question no one seems to want to ask is what the spiritual condition of the other 98 % is?**

I question whether anyone can be a genuine Christian without sharing, at least to some degree, our Lord's desire to see lost people saved. Jesus said He came to the world to *"seek and to save that which was lost."* (Luke 19:10) Therefore, if we are in Christ, and He in us, then He is seeking the lost through us, by giving us the desire to see them saved. Had someone not shared Christ with us, we would not be saved ourselves, and apart from the power of the indwelling Christ, we would have no desire to see others saved. But the reverse is also true; because of Christ, we are saved, and one of the evidences that our salvation experience was real is that He is now giving us the desire to see others saved.

That truth is validated in the life of the Apostle Paul. Paul's compassion for his people to be saved was the result of his own confessing of Jesus Christ as his personal Savior and Lord. Paul knew in his heart, that had it not been for that encounter with Jesus Christ on the road to Damascus, he would have remained lost and on his way to hell. But, when Paul confessed Jesus Christ as the Messiah, the Savior, the One sent from God to be our Redeemer, that dramatic event so changed his life that his heart's desire was to see those he loved saved as well.

Now, what is interesting here is to see that, while Paul's passion was to see his people saved, their passion was to see Paul suffer, if not die, as a result of his acceptance of Jesus Christ as the Messiah. They called him a liar, a false prophet; they beat him, cursed him, and locked him in stocks, chained to a wall, in a rat-infested dungeon. Wherever Paul went, the Jews, the very ones Paul was trying to see saved, would do their best to turn the people against him. And those who did receive Christ as their Savior were also taunted and belittled by those who opposed Paul.

So, how could Paul still have this passion to see them saved after all they had done to him? Where did that passion come from? Was it from human motives? Not hardly! Such a love is not a part of our human nature, regardless of how good we are.

Paul's passion for his people was the "fruit" of the Holy Spirit indwelling and empowering him. It came from the love God shed abroad in his heart the very instant He believed in Jesus. It was simply the outflow of his heart that had been filled with God's love for him. It was the irrefutable, unquestionable, undeniable evidence of his salvation.

It was the same passion for the lost that sent David Livingstone to blaze the trail through the wild bush of Africa, and Adoniram Judson into the jungles of Burma to carry the message of Jesus Christ to those who were lost. It was that same passion for the lost that motivated Elizabeth Elliott to go to the very spot where natives killed her husband, and to complete the mission he was sent to do; even leading to Christ the very man who put the spear into her husband's side.

It is that love for the lost that keeps our missionaries on their fields today, and preachers in their pulpits, and evangelists on their circuits. It is that same passion that is moving in the hearts of men, women, boys and girls to prepare themselves to be ready to take up the standard when the mantle of missions is handed down to them.

It was that same love that brought Jesus down from glory; to die on a cross so gory, yet as a sacrifice for the sin of every human being. It is a love which the waters of sorrow and suffering, grief and pain, rejection or neglect, or even death itself cannot quench. Rather, it is in these times that this kind of love grows stronger and stronger. As Paul said in 1 Corinthians 13, this kind of love never gives up, and this kind of love never fails. If that kind of love for the lost is in your heart today, it is because God put it there on the day He saved you by His grace. That love abides within you, through the indwelling presence of the Holy Spirit. Oh, but if that love for the lost is not there, how can you know for sure that even you are truly saved?

In Romans 9:1-2, Paul said he had a great *"heaviness and sorrow"* in his heart. That heaviness is what we might know as depression, and the Greek word used here for "sorrow" means an intense grief that is accompanied by tears. Paul went about in heaviness and sorrow over the lostness of those he loved. There was never a moment where he was not concerned for their eternal welfare. He said he even found himself wanting to trade places with them; wishing he could be separated from Christ himself, if doing so would bring his fellow Jews to the Lord.

Why is it that, as Christians today, we seem to be more concerned about the sins of the sinner than we are about the sinner? A sinner is just acting true to his nature, regardless of the sin he commits. He is not a sinner because he sins, but rather he sins because he is a sinner, just as we were before the grace of God. Through the death of Jesus Christ, God has shown us that He loved the sinner enough to do more for him than just to condemn him for acting true to his nature. He loved him enough to die for those sins.

When we see a sinner acting true to his nature, is our response in reaction to the sin, or in compassion for the sinner? What is our response to that down and out person who is living in sin, stealing from others, lying their way through life, having wasted their resources on drugs or alcohol; too lazy to assume personal responsibility for their actions, much less the welfare of their family, and they stand before us with their hand out?

What is our response to that person who appears to have it made, wearing the finest, driving the best, living high and mighty, and flaunting their sinful lifestyle and immoral behavior as if nothing was wrong with what they are doing, and they take the name of the Lord in vain, or voice some vulgar expletive that is offensive to our children?

What is our response to that person who just can't get it all together in life, always borrowing from others to make ends meet, always looking for the easy way out or blaming someone else for their lack of success, always wondering why they can't have what they want, and all the time they are telling you this, they are drinking and smoking and watching a less than acceptable program on TV?

Have we become so calloused to sin that we have no compassion for the sinner? Have we become so repulsed by their behavior and hardened by their haughty attitude that we have forgotten that they are being held captive to sin, just as we were before we were saved? Have we forgotten what it is like to be lost, without even a desire to be saved? Have we forgotten that we were once "dead in our trespasses and sins?" And, had it not been for God's intervention into our lives, we would still be as lost as we were before.

We are moved to tears as we see the hurt of those who live in war-torn countries, or the suffering of those whose lives have been ravaged by storms or other catastrophes, and well we should. But when was the last time you saw anyone moved to tears over the lostness of every man, woman, boy or girl who is not saved. When was the last time your church was on its knees in prayer, crying out unto God for the lost that live in your area, as well as those around the world?

In Acts 20:31, Paul reminded his brethren that for three years he *"did not cease to warn everyone night and day, with tears."* In Hebrews 5:7, the writer refers to Jesus, our High Priest, who *"offered up prayers and supplications, with strong crying and tears."* The prophet Isaiah said the Messiah would be a *"man of sorrows and acquainted with grief."* Mark said: *"Jesus saw a great multitude, and was moved with compassion for them, because they were like sheep, not having s shepherd."* (Mark 6:34) And Matthew wrote about Jesus, looking over the city of Jerusalem, and crying out unto God: *"O Jerusalem, Jerusalem...how oft I wanted to gather your children together, as a hen gathers her chicks under her wings."* (Matthew 23:37)

General William Booth, the founder of the Salvation Army, was a man of passion for God and compassion for the lost. One day he received a letter from one of his young captains who had not seen any response to his messages on redemption. Booth, known to be a man of few words, sent that young minister a telegram of two words: "Try Tears!"

I see churches trying so many things to "attract" lost people to their church facilities, rather than sending their folks out to where the lost folks are living. Church growth specialists call these events "bridges" or "entrances" into the church, through which an unbeliever can become involved in church activities, fellowship with church people, be exposed to the gospel, and hopefully be saved. So churches are conducting or sponsoring events that address some of the "life-need issues" of the lost – marriage and the family, finances, parenting skills, divorce recovery, youth issues, men's issues, women's issues, even addressing some of their secular needs as well, such as resume' writing, English as a second language, car maintenance and repair, to name a few. While these methods have been helpful, useful and beneficial to the participants, and perhaps offered them some very valuable information, the problem is that we haven't seen much lasting fruit from them, in terms of real evangelism.

Other churches employ the "big event" method of reaching out to the lost, and some of them are quite successful in getting the lost on the church grounds or into the church facility. Some offer weekend seminars with well-known speakers, seasonal choir concerts with colorful pageantry and dramatic activity. One of the mega-churches estimated that, over a three-day period, some 15,000 unchurched people attended one of their seasonal events, filled out the response card, and expressed an interest in knowing more about the church and what it means to be a Christian. But, according to one of the staff members, in the 90 days that followed, there was no measurable difference in their Sunday School or worship attendance or in the number of baptisms, and no indication that any of those 15,000 people were still coming to their church. My question is how can a church justify such a major expenditure if there are no "net" results?

As we said in the earlier chapters of this book, some churches are adjusting their Sunday morning services to "attract" lost people to their services. Their thought is, by removing the barriers of tradition, softening the messages on sin, relaxing their standards of dress codes, formality and function, and by using a music style that sounds like the music lost people listen to, that they will feel comfortable in church, and will want to become a part of the family. It is a good thought; perhaps well intentioned, but wrong.

Several years ago, God convicted me regarding my own passion for the lost. In so many words, the Lord asked me if I was really concerned about the lives of those who were lost, or was I just trying to improve my baptismal scorecard and church growth records?

At that time I was also going through a study on the essentials of expository preaching, and the necessity of such preaching if the lost are to be saved and the saved are to grow in the grace and knowledge of the Lord. Needless to say, such conviction caused a real change in my prayer life, as well as in my methods of evangelism and discipleship.

I would suspect that question would bring a lot of conviction upon a lot of pastors today, as we seem to be more concerned about growing the church through attendance than we are in adding to the Kingdom of God, those whom the Lord is calling to be saved, through our witness. We may be gaining "attendance" through all of our efforts, but it is very obvious that we are not making a difference in the lives of lost people, nor are we making a dent in the numbers of lost people who now live in America.

It seems to me that the church has tried, and is trying about every method known to man to reach the lost. **Maybe it is time we tried tears!** Our concern for the lost, whether it is within our own family, our own neighborhood, or in some area in the world no one else will bother with, is not a matter of emotional stirrings or perhaps even the guilt that some may be feeling after reading this chapter. Our concern for the lost is the activity of the Holy Spirit who dwells in our heart, and whose purpose is to conform us to the image of Jesus Christ. And the more we increase our intimacy with God, through our study of His Word, the more we learn of the real meaning of the cross, and of the value God places on one human soul, as well as the eternal doom that awaits those who refuse his offer of eternal salvation.

But we will also learn of the loss which will be ours at the judgment seat of Christ when we come before Him empty handed, or of the great reward which will be ours on that day when we stand before Christ with the crowds of those we have either witnessed to personally, or provided the witness for them through some other way. If that day was today, what would your judgment be?

But just as there is a deep concern on my heart to see lost people saved, there is an equal burden, if not even a greater one, to see those who are saved discipled until they can walk by faith, being able to understand the Word of God and growing through their consistent study of it, but also being able to share their faith, and to teach others the Word of God.

In *My Utmost for His Highest*, Oswald Chambers wrote:

> *"Our work begins where God's grace has laid the foundation; we are not to save souls, but to disciple them. Salvation and sanctification are the work of God's sovereign grace; our work as His disciples is to disciple lives unto they are wholly yielded to God. One life wholly devoted to God is of more value to God than one hundred lives simply awakened by His Spirit. God brings us to a standard of life by His grace, and we are responsible for reproducing that standard in others."* (*My Utmost For His Highest*, Discovery House Publishers, 1935)

The reason this burden for discipleship is so strong in my heart is because of the lack of real discipleship in my own experience with Christ in those precious early years. I was saved at the age of nine. While I did not know all there was to know about salvation, of course, much less deep theology and biblical history, I knew my life had been radically changed, and that something different was happening in my heart. Having had the assignment in Bible College to go back and trace those steps that led up to my experience with Christ, I know beyond a shadow of a doubt that Jesus Christ came into my life, forgave me of my sin, and gave me a new purpose and a new vision of what He wanted me to be. No, I was not always obedient to that vision, but I know I was saved.

What saddens me is that I was 28 years old before I fully understood that I could not live the Christian life in my own strength. But, if I would die to myself completely, then God would inhabit me wholly, and Christ could live His life through me fully, to accomplish, through me, what He would do Himself, if He was here to do it. In other words, I was almost 20 years old in the faith before I began to understand the freedom and power of Galatians 2:20.

The truth was, I didn't know any more about the Bible or how to understand it when I was 28 years old than I did when I was 9 years old. I didn't know any more about prayer, or about the purpose of the church, the doctrines of our faith, the traditions of our faith, or why the church did or did not do something, etc., than I did when I was first saved. For almost 20 years, I lived without the full assurance of my salvation. And, as a result of that, I don't ever remember sharing my testimony with anyone, not even my kinfolk.

Then, three men began to disciple me about the things of God and the ways of God. For over a year, they taught me how to grow in the grace and the knowledge of God's Word through a consistent and disciplined study of God's Word;

how to pray in the power of the Holy Spirit, and how to live out those things that God was putting into my life each day, beginning with my own wife and son, and our extended families. Before long, we were not only learning how to do this for ourselves, we were also teaching others how they could do the same things.

Since those days, my wife and I have opened our hearts and our home to anyone who truly wants to be discipled in their walk with the Lord. In every church where Linda and I have served, we opened our hearts and our home to those who wanted to be discipled. As a Pastor, I had to open it up to anyone, lest it appear that I was playing favorites with some of the church members. But I knew when the requirements were made clear, many of those who said they wanted to "attend" would excuse themselves because of other commitments, and we understood that.

For years we used a tool called *Master Life*, written by Avery Willis and produced through the Southern Baptist Sunday School Board (now Lifeway). Later, we began to develop our own process, especially with those who wanted to move beyond the basic discipleship material. We took each person where they were in their journey of faith, and walked with them, almost step by step, until they could walk by faith; assured of their salvation, knowing the will of God for their lives, able to discern, understand and apply the Word of God, seeing real answers to their prayers, being passionate about sharing their faith with others, and involved in the discipleship of others

Recently we had the joy of a brief reunion with one of those who was in one of our first discipleship groups. She and her husband, who was also in that group, are now very involved in various leadership positions in their local church, having poured their lives into hundreds of young adults over the years, and now into their own two children. When we began to talk about our days of discipleship with them she said *"Hardly a week goes by without someone asking them where they learned some of the biblical principles they have adopted for their lives, and we are quick to tell them that it was in a discipleship group over 30 years ago."* She continued *"The basic truths you taught us and lived before us became personal convictions for our lives. We have not only lived by them, we have been blessed by them, and we have shared them with others, as the Lord has given us opportunity."*

Some of those we discipled heard the call of God and are now serving the Lord in their local churches in the United States. Others were called to serve as missionaries around the world, or to serve as godly lay-workers in their churches, or spouses of those who do. And the greatest joy of our heart is to hear how they are continuing the process by sharing some of those same principles we taught them with their life-mates, their children, their friends, as well as with those they lead to the Lord. As the Apostle John said *"I rejoiced greatly that I found of thy children walking in truth!"* (2 John 1:4)

In 1998, Linda and I were attending a conference in Atlanta and we discovered there were people there from almost every discipleship group we had ever started since 1974 in that same conference. We didn't plan it, but God brought us together to confirm the method of ministry He ordained to be used in the local church – discipleship. It will work if we will do it the way God said we are to do it. Yes, it will require the sacrifice of our personal lives, just as our salvation required the personal sacrifice of our Lord. Was our life worth His? Isn't our life worth theirs, and those they will reach for Christ? The work of the church can fall apart in one generation if we fail to pass on to others that which has been passed down to us. Are you passing it down to others who will be able to teach others also, including your children? The Great Commission was not a mandate for world-wide evangelism but our Lord's command to continue the process of discipleship.

The Apostle Paul used this type of ministry as he started those first churches years ago. He would enter a town and start teaching in the synagogues or in areas where he could gather a crowd. He would share the gospel of Jesus Christ with those who would listen, and preach his heart out until the religious leaders forced him to leave. Then Paul would look around to see who was still standing beside him, supporting him and believing in what he had preached to them, and he would take those faithful few and begin to establish a church around them. He would put one of them in charge until one of his own men could come and give it support, structure, and teach them the Word of God.

In every church Paul started, he used this same method of reproducing himself in the lives of those who would reproduce themselves in the lives of others. So, it is no wonder, as Paul neared the end of his life, that he gave this message to Timothy, his son in the Lord, that he must do the same thing. Timothy was to take the things he had learned from Paul and teach them to those who would then be faithful to teach them to others. Jesus called it discipleship – teaching others to observe the things the Lord is teaching us.

Timothy had not only heard the gospel from the lips of the Apostle Paul, he had also seen it fleshed out in Paul's life. Timothy traveled with Paul on many of his journeys, and he heard him preach and teach the Word of God too many different kinds of people; some who could have cared less about what they were hearing, as well as those new believers who wanted to hear all they could about the love of Christ.

Timothy had heard all of the wonderful, marvelous truths of the gospel of Jesus Christ, and He had seen the impact those words had had on the various groups of people. Paul's words brought hope and new life to those who were hungry for truth, and at the same time, they brought despair and death to those who were offended by them. Timothy had seen the opposition Paul suffered and the hurt that Paul endured just to preach the gospel. But he also saw the tremendous blessing that came to those who believed in what they heard, and the life change that took place in those who trusted in what Paul had said and received Jesus Christ as their Savior and Lord.

Through it all, Timothy had learned the pure doctrine of salvation, by grace, through faith in Jesus Christ, plus nothing. Day after day, he had heard it from Paul's lips, and he had seen it in Paul's life, and he knew it was real. Perhaps more than any other man in his day, Timothy had seen the power of God confirming the Word of God as he watched the life of his teacher live by the very grace of God he was preaching about.

But the spiritual heritage that Timothy had been so privileged to experience needed to be more than just good memories, or entries in his journal; it was to be considered a sacred trust. Whatever Timothy had seen or heard or learned from Paul, he was to guard it as a treasure which had been entrusted to him. But he was not to hoard it to himself, so as to become puffed up with spiritual pride. He was to pass it on, but not just to anyone. Like Paul, Timothy would teach and preach to everyone in the congregation. But then he would seek out those whom God would point out to him as those who would keep the process going from generation to generation. This was Paul's method of multiplication, and to some degree, you and I are hearing these wonderful truths today because Timothy passed them on to others who then passed them on to us.

Someone said **the process of evangelism is not complete until the evangelized become evangelists!** I believe this is what Jesus meant when he said, *"Go into all the world and make disciples!"* (Matthew 28:18) He did not say, lead them to Christ and then leave them alone to fend for themselves. He said, *"Teach them to observe all things whatsoever I have commanded you!"* (Matthew 28:20) Very simply put, "Fellows, you go tell others what I have told you! And remember, I will always be with you"!

Somehow we have changed the process from "multiplication" to "additions", and we aren't getting the gospel out as quick and effective as we could and should be doing. Let's assume the world's population is 4 billion, 500 million, give or take a few million. And, let's suppose a man wanted to reach the world with the gospel of Jesus Christ by preaching to as many people as he could in his lifetimes. So, he says he is going to preach to 1,000 people every day of his life, and he organizes a group of helpers to go into each town and set up his meetings.

So, without a day off, this man continues his preaching to the thousands throughout the year – 365,000 each year. What preacher wouldn't be happy with that kind of attendance? But as this rate, it will take him 10,958 years just to reach the world, assuming there would be no population growth at all.

But if we were using the multiplication method that Jesus designed, and that Paul used so effectively, we could get the whole Word to the whole world in our lifetime. If one person, living in an average size community would share his faith with his neighbors and friends until he found three others who were willing to develop their faith and share it with others, the multiplication process would begin. Over the next year, that one person would show these other three persons how to study their Bible, how to pray, how to share their testimony, and how to share the gospel. He would give them a Christian world view, and then, at the end of that year, send them off to share their faith with the multitudes, until they find their three disciples, and the multiplication process continues.

At the end of the first year, there are 9, but in another year there are 27. At the end of the fourth year there are 81, and at the end of the fifth year 243. If that process continued for 21 consecutive years, the gospel of Jesus Christ would be shared with 10 billion, 460 million, 353 thousand, 203 people, and the multiplication process would be well on its way of fulfilling the great commission. The key to the process is finding those faithful men who will pass it on to others.

But not only should we disciple them as far as our spiritual heritage, but we should also instruct them in regard to the history of the Christian Church from Acts 2:42 until now. We owe it to those who want to become a part of the fellowship of the church, to explain the history of the local church, its particular denomination, how it began, and what distinguishes it from the other denominations, especially between Protestant and Catholic. I believe this would include an overview of all confessions, covenants and commitments; anything that would explain what the church believes, doctrinally, theologically and practically, including their responsibility to the church regarding attendance, leadership, stewardship and ministry. And this should be done before they are accepted as members.

We also need to instruct them regarding the historical significance of the Bible, the accepted ordinances of Baptism and the Lord's Supper, as well as any specific traditions that set that church body apart from others. I believe each new church member should be provided a copy of the church constitution, bylaws, and any materials that would illustrate their core values, their mission statement, and their plans for accomplishing that vision. Included in that should be a brief biography of their pastors and ministerial staff members, past as well as present. Again, we owe it to those who are considering joining our churches to tell them – this is how we began, this is where we have come from, this is who we are and where we are, and this is where we are going in the future.

Over the past few years, church membership has lost its meaning. Church members are not only allowed, but have been encouraged to change their membership from church to church, depending upon what is "happening" in the various churches. There is very little, if any commitment to a church family – to stick together, through the good times and the bad, the seasons of high praise and the years of struggle. We have forgotten Paul's admonition in Ephesians 4:2, which says:

> *"With all lowliness and meekness, with longsuffering,...forbearing one another in love; endeavoring to keep the unity of the Spirit in the bond of peace. There is one body, and one Spirit, even as ye are called in one hope of your calling; One Lord, one faith, one baptism, one God and Father of all, who is above all, and through all, and in you all."* (Ephesians 4:2)

All believers are united into one body the very moment they are born again; saved by the grace of God. That glorious body, of which Christ is the Head (Ephesians 4:14-16), is called the Universal Church; the elect of God – all those who have ever and who will ever believe in the name of the Lord are adopted into that family without prejudice or impartiality. Peter referred to each one as *"lively stones...built up {into a} spiritual house, a holy priesthood, to offer up sacrifices, acceptable to God by Jesus Christ."* (1 Peter 2:4) He continues, *"But ye are a chosen generation, a royal priesthood, a holy nation, a peculiar people; that ye should show forth the praises of him who hath called you out of darkness into his marvelous light; which in times past were not a people, but are now the people of God."* (1 Peter 2:9-10)

I believe it is time to raise the standard of church

membership, not continue to lower it. When we think of the supreme sacrifice the Lord Jesus made to unite all believers into one body, as well as the personal sacrifices thousands of others have made in establishing the church, not only in the proclamation of the gospel, but also in the preservation of the truth, how dare we cheapen that which cost many of them their very lives? Being a member of a local church is a wonderful privilege, but also a tremendous responsibility. Our purpose ought to be to keep the church pure, undiluted by false doctrine and false teachings, unspoiled with hypocrisy and vain religion. If we will do that, the Lord Himself will do what only He can do; *"add to the church daily such as should be saved."* (Acts 2:47)

CHAPTER EIGHT

The Raising of the Standard In Our Love for the Family

Until the day our Lord returns to this earth, the Church is to be His Body in the world. Therefore, as those who make up His Body, it is our responsibility to live our lives in such a way that the rest of the world can see the righteousness of Christ in us against the backdrop of the unrighteousness of the world, and be drawn to Jesus as their Savior. In 1 Peter 2:11-12, the Apostle said, *"Dearly beloved, I beseech you as strangers and pilgrims, abstain from fleshly lusts, which war against the soul; Having your conversation honest among the gentiles; that, whereas they speak against you as evildoers, they may BY YOUR GOOD WORKS, which they shall behold, GLORIFY GOD in the day of visitation."* (Emphasis mine)

But the main reason we are seeing the rise of evil and the acceptance of sin in our society today is because the members of the church have allowed the standard of the Lord fall into disgrace by our own immorality. Consequently, if we ever expect to see a return to the values and virtues that once set this nation apart from all of the others, as being the one nation, blessed of God, then true revival must begin in the church. In 1 Peter 4:17, the Apostle said, *"For the time is come that judgment must begin at the house of God; and if it first begin in us, what shall the end be of them that obey not the gospel of God?"*

I believe the most crucial standard we have allowed to fall into disgrace is the God-given institution of marriage and the family. God Himself ordained the family as the foundational institution of the world – not the government, not the community, not a village, not even the church or any religious organization. The basic unit of our society is the family. History confirms the old adage: as goes the family, so goes the church, the community, the state, and eventually, the nation.

But this most sacred and significant institution may soon be extinct. Today, married couples average having only 1.4 children per household, when only a few years ago it was 2.5. While we have seen some reduction in the number of abortions, it is still one out of every three and that is one too many. One day our nation will give an account of every unborn child that has been murdered in the womb. Even our President, who strongly opposes abortion personally, says the moral climate in America is still not right to push for a constitutional amendment prohibiting abortion, except in cases of rape, incest or when the life of the mother is in danger. God help us.

But not only is something as foundational and fundamental as the marriage union and the family unit being threatened socially, it is also being challenged legally, morally, and Biblically. The personal agenda of the homosexual activists is very clear. Their desire is to rid our society of every restraint of sexual decency, by removing the laws that protect the sanctity of the marriage union as being between one man and one woman, or else by rescinding those laws that prohibit same-sex marriages from being legal. In many states, laws against sodomy are already on the books, but they are not being enforced. To add insult to injury, many of those who are leading the charge against the traditional marriage call themselves "priests" who either see this as an issue of "love" rather than "law" or who are practicing homosexuals themselves. How can anyone read the Word of God without recognizing homosexuality as an abomination against God? (Leviticus 18:22)

In 1998, messengers from the Southern Baptist Churches assembled in Salt Lake City, Utah for their annual convention. During the meeting, a statement was added to the Baptist Faith and Message regarding the sanctity of marriage and the family, in essence to make a stand against homosexual marriages. Reading the editorials in the major newspapers the next day, one would have thought that Southern Baptists had voted to treat women as slaves, rather than lifting them up to the exalted level as outlined in God's Word. A copy of that statement has been included as an addendum to this book for your review. I submit to you, there is not one word of content or intent in that statement that cannot be validated either by command, precept or example in the Bible. And yet, some of the greatest protests came from those within the Christian community.

The problem we are facing today in our marriages and in our families stems from an abysmal failure in the highest office of the land. No, I'm not referring to the office of the Presidency; I'm speaking about the God-ordained office of husband and father. If we are going to make a difference in the world we are leaving to our children, then men, husbands and dads must assume their God-given responsibility as spiritual leaders of their marriage and their family. I believe our wives and our children are ready to follow men who are, unashamedly following Jesus Christ.

One does not have to be a prophet to see the destruction that lies ahead for our children if we continue to travel down the road to ruin we are on today. In a recent television expose', it was revealed how deviant sexual activity is on the rise among our children and youth. The saddest part was that the children and youth saw it as "no big deal – it's just sex" they said. The standards of decency and morality have been lowered so far that there is no shame, no guilt, and no conviction of sin for having sex outside of marriage.

History warns us that no society has ever survived that allowed homosexuality to become an acceptable lifestyle. **And unless we raise the standard of honorable marriage and family in the church today, it may not be more than one generation until the sanctity of marriage will be no more.** Those who would argue with that statement need to review what has already happened to the sanctity of human life regarding the unborn, and what is about to happen regarding the aged as well.

Over 40 years ago, our nation played the prodigal with God's most precious gift to us: the family. We took the inheritance of our faith that was handed down to us by our parents and grandparents, at the cost of great sacrifice on their part, and we squandered it in search of a better way of life than we thought we had at home. At the beginning, it appeared that this new experiment would work, as this new prosperity provided for our every dream. Each day, new ways were introduced to help us have a family, just like our parents and grandparents had, yet live the kind of selfish lives we wanted to live. Books were written, seminars were offered and television programs were produced to help both parents balance the demands of career and home, and to do it without guilt.

But the pursuit of wealth and the accumulation of material things began to take its toll on the unity of the family. The parents' desire for independence turned into rebellion on the part of the children and teenagers. They all lived under the same roof, but they lived their own lives, in their own private areas; not as a family unit, not even at meal time. As a result, there was no love, no warmth, no real oneness between them, no real need for each other – no family, as God intended it to be.

All of the benefits we thought we were providing for our children somehow could not salve our broken hearts as we watched them search for love and attention in the daycare center, or in the after-school programs in the community. The guilt of having abandoned our children for the sake of material prosperity caused many couples to re-evaluate their priorities of life, and to make the necessary changes to raise their families in the way of the Lord. Some did not, and their families still suffer from it today.

God places a high value on the family unit, not only because it is where each child can learn about real life from and through those who dearly love them, but also because it is through this relationship that real faith in God is to be passed down from generation to generation. While the organized church may assist in this process, and it should, the real responsibility for this transfer of truth rests upon the family, especially the fathers. It is the lack of that transfer over the past two generations that is causing such a dilemma in the church today.

Without justifying their actions, this may be the reason why the contemporary church feels the need to always bring the preaching and teaching down to its lowest level. The majority of those church members who are under 40 years of age did not get that transfer of truth from their parents, or from the church. That is why they find it difficult to comprehend deeper spiritual issues; they were not rooted and grounded in the basic, fundamental truths of God's Word. This is why they want everything para-phrased, bite-sized, adjusted to their tastes and styles, media-driven, entertaining, and couched in phrases and slogans they can understand – they have not "grown up" in the Word, because their parents failed to pass it down to them.

In the introduction to his book, *"A Better Way"* Michael Horton said: *"it will take an entire generation of reeducation in the substance of the Christian faith and practice for us to attain linguistic competence again."* (A Better Way, Baker Books, a division of Baker Publishing Group, 2002) While I would wholeheartedly agree with that statement, unless today's generation of parents see the error of their ways and return to the ways of God, I'm not sure there will be anyone to reeducate by the end of the next generation.

In the book of Exodus, Moses reminded us of how the children of Israel were delivered from their slavery in Egypt, but then failed to be obedient to God as the approached the Promised Land. As a result, they were sent to the desert for 40 years, and everyone in that generation died because of their lack of faith in and obedience to God.

In the book of Deuteronomy, which means "second law", or the second time around, Moses is facing a new generation of Israelites. For the second time, the people of God are about to enter Canaan and take the land God had promised to their forefathers, and Moses is literally laying the law down to them as to how it must be if they want to receive God's blessings. Deuteronomy 6:4-9, along with Deuteronomy 11:13-21 and Numbers 15:37-41, are known as the *Shema*, which became Judaism's basic confession of faith. According to Rabbinic law, these verses were to be recited morning and night.

> *"Thou shalt teach them diligently unto thy children, and shall talk of them when thou sittest in thine house, and when thou walkest by the way, and when thou liest down, and when thou risest up. And thou shalt bind them for a sign upon thine hand, and they shall be as frontlets between thine eyes. And thou shalt write them upon the doorposts of thy house, and on thy gates."* (Deuteronomy 6:7-9)

The admonition was not only for the adults to memorize and mediate upon the law of God, but to continually expose their children to God's laws and commandments. Some of the Jewish people took literally, and they placed a copy of the Shema in a small metal box and attached it near their main entrance. It was called a "mezuzah" which means door post, and each family member touched that little box every time they entered or exited the home, as a reminder of their need to be obedient unto God.

But Deuteronomy 6:20 is the most crucial text for our subject matter here. It is as if Moses is predicting what would happen, so the parents would be forced to transfer their faith down to their children. He said: *"And when thy son asketh thee in time to come, saying, what mean the testimonies, and the statutes, and the judgments, which the Lord our God hath commanded you? Then thou shalt say unto thy son"*...and Moses recites the wonderful story of God's deliverance of His people from Egyptian slavery.

Deuteronomy 6:23-25 are such powerful verses, I must include them here. Moses said:

> *"And he (God) brought us out from thence, that he might bring us in, to give us the land which he sware unto our fathers. And the Lord commanded us to do all these statutes, to fear the Lord our God, for our good always, that he might preserve us alive, as it is at this day. And it shall be our righteousness if we observe to do all these commandments before the Lord our God, as he hath commanded us."*

Of course their outward obedience to God's laws did not guarantee them eternal life, but it did give them the right to the land. What a testimony for them to share with their children.

In this wonderful passage of Holy Scripture, Moses told

the Israelites, if they wanted it to go well with them when they went in to possess the land God had given them, (vs 18), and if they wanted to survive as a nation (vs 24), they must continue to transfer their faith in the God of their fathers, down to their children, and to their children's children. They had to teach their children to *"Observe these statutes; to fear the Lord our God!"*

There are three principles outlined in this brief text that show us how God intended that transfer of truth to be carried out:

1. The parents were to permeate their heart with the love of God. (Vs 5-6)

> *"You shall love the Lord your God with all your heart and with all your soul and with all your might. And these words, which I am commanding you today, shall be on your heart."* (NASB)

Well, here we are at the first chapter of this book again. We have come full circle in our search for the place(s) we have let the standard of our Lord fall into disgrace, and here it is again – *"thou shalt love the Lord thy God with all thine heart, soul and mind!"* Even Jesus said it was the first and greatest commandment. So that means this commandment was not only for the children of Israel in that day, it is for the children of God in our day.

Parents, is your heart permeated with the love of God? Can you say right now that you love God with ALL your heart; ALL your soul: ALL your mind or might? Can your children and your grandchildren see that? Is it obvious to them that God alone is YOUR God – the captain of your mind – the One you obey – the One in whom you trust, and the One to whom you pray? If we don't let them know that, and see that, how will they learn about OUR God, and know that He is the One in whom they also should believe? With all due respect, that is not the responsibility of the church; that is a charge given to the parents. And the sad reality is, the concept of God we see in the lives of our children and youth today is the concept they see in the lives of their parents today, and the concept of God that was handed down to them from the past generations. The principle works for the good or for the bad and God wants us to use it for good in the lives of our children.

2. Parents are to saturate their children's heart with the love of God – (Vs 7)

"And you shall teach them diligently." (NASB)

The word "diligently" means to impress the truth upon them with great intensity. Someone is going to impress their concept of life upon the mind of every little child. God's plan is for it to be their godly parents, and He gave us two ways for this to be done.

The first is **verbally** – *"Talk of them when you sit in your house and when you walk by the way, and when you lie down and when you rise up!"(vs 7)* God said parents are to talk to their children about the love of God as a part of their normal conversation at home. That doesn't mean a parent has to quote Bible verses in the King James language, but it does mean that whatever is said, in the normal routine of life, should reflect the love of God which has been shed abroad in our own hearts.

It means that as many times in the day as possible, both Dad and Mom take their precious little child, hold it in their arms, and tell them over and over how much they love them, and how much God loves them. It mean you plan the mealtime with the children, and use those times to talk about the things God has done for the family, and how He blessed you in some way that day. It means setting aside some specific time for each teenager, finding out where they are in their walk with the Lord, and discovering some ways to encourage them in their journey of faith. It means planning a time when the whole family gets together for prayer and Bible study; letting the children see your dependence upon the Word of God for your own source of truth, and in prayer as your own source of strength and power. It means making sure that whatever is going on in that home is constantly teaching the children about the love of God for them; that they truly are "precious in His sight" and that you are grateful for the opportunity to be their parents.

But then there are some ***non-verbal ways*** of sharing your faith with your children. (vs. 8-9). We have already mentioned the "mezuzah" that little metal box that contained the "Shema" which was attached to the right-hand doorpost at every entrance to the home. Each family member would touch that little box each time they entered or exited the home, as a reminder that their home was a household of faith. The Hebrew men would copy these four verses of the law, put them in a little leather case and bind them to their wrists and to their foreheads during the morning and evening prayer. Everywhere that child turned, they would be reminded of their parents' faith and trust in the God who loved them, and they could not get away from that.

The practical principle here is for parents to demonstrate their devotion to God by the appearance of the home. If parents want to raise their children to live their lives in the center of God's perfect will, then their home must be centered in the things of God and not in the world. What do your children see in your home that points them to God? What impressions are left on their minds as they leave that home every morning and return every evening? Sooner or later, our children will learn who and what our "god" really is, and more often it will not be by what we say, but how we live.

3. Parents should validate their children's faith when they start to ask questions – (vs 20-25)

"When your son asks you, IN TIME TO COME, saying, what do these testimonies and the statutes and the judgments mean..." (NASB – Emphasis mine)

Sooner or later, sons and daughters are going to ask their parents why they do things a certain way. Why do they dress differently from other parents down the street? Why don't they have all the nice things other families have? Why won't they let them do some of the things other parents let their children do? Why do they insist they attend church every Sunday when most other parents don't even go themselves?

If a parent only sees those questions as being obstinate or rebellious, and just gives their children some sort of surface answer, they will have missed a great opportunity to share the foundational principle of their faith in God. Moses said, parents should use this teachable moment to share their own personal testimony of how they were saved, why they love the Lord so much, and how that experience so radically changed their lives. In other words, it is at this very moment that a parent should stop whatever he or she is doing, and give that child the "reason for the hope that is within them!" For this is where their faith in God, their trust in the Word of God, and the values of life they have derived from that faith will be validated. This is where the parent passes down to their children what true faith in God is all about.

Parents, our children, and especially our teenagers may argue with the commandments, the laws, the statutes and the restrictions of God's Word, because it hampers their personal freedom. But they cannot argue with a changed life, especially if it is someone they truly love, and someone who truly loves them. And, while they may not embrace your faith in God at that very moment, you have done your part. You have shared the Word of God, and validated it with your life. The rest is up to their response to the work of the Holy Spirit in their lives, and the only thing left for us to do is pray.

This is God's purpose for the family, and those who have been, and still are trying to destroy the family know it, which is why they seem to be hell-bent on carrying out their evil plot. We are living in the first generation of Americans who do not have a godly heritage. The majority of people under the age of 30 do not have the same kind of foundation of faith that most of us over the age of 50 had as children, and therefore they cannot pass down to their children that which they did not receive from their parents.

Therefore, children today don't know what it is like to have godly role models in every area of their lives, the schools, the grocery, the bank, the gas stations, even the major sporting events. They don't know what it is like to live on a safe street or to go to sleep and leave the doors unlocked. They don't know the joys of a simple walk through a park or to sit on the top of a mountain and dream. They don't understand the basic principles of life, such as decency, honesty, integrity and morality, which is why they don't know the difference between love and lust. They don't know what it was like when right was right and wrong was wrong; when truth was truth and a lie was a lie, regardless of who said it or did it. They don't understand why we say that every human life is precious, more valuable than anything in this world. They don't have the same fear of God, or for the judgment to come. Why? Because 50 years ago we abandoned God's concept of the family: a father and a mother and their own children, by birth or adoption. Today, only 1 in 6 children are being raised in that type of home, and that includes many Christian homes as well – **we have allowed the standard of the family fall into disgrace.**

Many parents are losing the battle with their children because they are fighting it out on the ground, when the real battle is in the air. In Ephesians 6:13-18, the Apostle Paul said our battle is not physical, meaning it is not with flesh and blood, including those within our family, and those who are trying to destroy the family. Our battle is spiritual! We are fighting the same principalities and powers of darkness that have tried to rule the world since Satan himself was cast out of heaven for his rebellion against God. We aren't going to Christianize the world our children live in – the schools, the entertainment centers, the media outlets, the clothing manufacturers, etc…we have been trying to do that for 50 years. It hasn't worked, and we don't have time for that kind of battle anymore.

We are in a battle for the hearts and minds of our children. It is warfare like we have never had before, at least in my lifetime. The evil world is spending billions of dollars trying to impress its value system upon our children, and it's doing a good job of warping their minds against God and the things of God. But God said we could save our children from such demonic powers if we will spend the time necessary to impress upon them the truth of God's Word, and the love God desires to give them. God said we can do that by showing them our own love for God in the way we invest our time, our money and our lives, and by just letting that love of God so permeate our lives that it spills out on our precious children. Then, God said our homes should be designed in such a way that His eternal values are visibly communicated to our children in every way they turn.

As a pastor, I have seen the devastation that is caused by divided families, not only upon the children within the divided family, but in their children's children as well.

But I have also seen God bestow some wonderful blessings upon those parents who were willing to pay the price to raise their children according to God's plan. Some placed their children in Christian schools, others turned to home school, and others just got more involved in their public or private schools. In most cases, it was not the method they chose, that determined the outcome of their children, but it was their own investment of time, energy, care and compassion. They did not relegate their secular education to the schools or their spiritual education to the church, but rather they assumed personal responsibility for their children's welfare, and God honored the desires of their heart.

If we are going to raise the standard of the Lord in our world today, it must begin in the home, with Dad and Mom, and then to each child or teenager. Yes, the price of change will be high, but so will the value of the difference it will make, not only in our lives, but in the lives of children for generations to come. The truth is, even many Christians have allowed the world to squeeze us into its mold. **But it is time for God's people to not only raise the standard of the family for their own sake, but to set the standard for the family for the rest of the world to see.** It used to be that way, even in America. It still can be, if parents are willing to walk away from the ways of the world, and stand up for the Lord.

CHAPTER NINE

The Raising of the Standard Of The Lord Jesus Christ

Centuries before Jesus Christ came to this earth, the prophets preached against the spiritual corruption, religious formalism and material prosperity of God's people. Like a mirror of our own age, the people of Israel totally disregarded their responsibility to set a higher standard of righteousness in their lives. God would tolerate their wickedness for a season, and then His hand of discipline, and outright judgment would fall.

There was a time in Israel's history when the people of God became extremely immoral and rebellious, thinking God had abandoned them. As a result of their disobedience to God's will and God's ways, they had been captives of the nation of Babylon for many years, and they longed to return to their beloved homeland of Israel and to worship again in Jerusalem. King Cyrus conquered Babylon, and the Jews saw this as a sign from God that He was going to set them free and send them home. But when that freedom was delayed, the Jews began to question God's concern for them, and rather than accept responsibility for their own sin, they began to blame God for allowing them to be taken captive. They became even more rebellious against God, thinking He had abandoned them, rather than them abandoning Him.

God called the prophet Isaiah to tell the people of Israel that it was not God's lack of desire or power to save them that had caused them to remain in their bondage; but their sin had separated them from God, and was causing them to feel as though He had abandoned them. Isaiah told them, if they would repent of their sins and turn back to God, the Holy Spirit would **raise up the standard within them,** and He (the Standard) would set them free. That is the central message of Isaiah 59, speaking prophetically of the second coming of Jesus Christ upon this earth, to rule and to reign as King of Kings and Lord of Lords for 1000 years.

In Isaiah 59:1-8, God, speaking through the prophet Isaiah said *"Behold the Lord's hand is not shortened that it cannot save; neither his ear heavy that it cannot hear; But your iniquities have separated between you and your God, and your sins have hid his face from you, that He will not hear."*

The Hebrew people were so angry with God for allowing them to be held captive that they were committing every vile and wicked sin known to man:

- In verse 3, the prophet said they sacrificed their firstborn children to the god of Moloch and killed the prophets whom God sent to warn them of the consequences of their rebellious behavior.
- Verse 4 says they perverted the justice system so they could get rid of certain people. No one demanded or even expected the truth to be told in a court case. They confused the courts with false testimony and

- legal wrangling that only brought more confusion and mistrust.
- Verse 5 says they spent all their time devising ways to catch someone in a trap, and they laughed when their trap took a person's life. There was absolutely no respect for human life as being the most expressive gift of God's creative power.
- Verses 6-8 say their works were evil and were meant to mislead or cheat each other –like selling woven spider-webs for silk. Their every thought was of iniquity and they looked for things to destroy. And to add insult to injury, they trained their children to follow their evil ways. And yet they wondered why God would not hear their prayers, deliver them from their captors and return them to their homeland

But the prophet Isaiah called the people together to hear the Word of God. And in no uncertain terms, Isaiah assured them that the problem was not with God, but with the people of God. He said there was no shortness in God's arms that He could not deliver them; there was nothing wrong with God's ears that prevented Him from hearing their prayers. But it was their gross, vile and wicked sin that separated Him from them and was causing Him to turn His face from them.

I believe we would all agree that the church is in the same condition today as the nation of Israel was in the days of Isaiah. I know many pastors, as well as many laymen, who are crying out for God to intervene and to deliver us from our own iniquities. I have been in prayer meetings where some of God's most respected saints have cried out for God's supernatural power to be released upon this nation, and against the powers of darkness and the forces of evil. But it is as though the ceilings are of brass and the heavens of steel, for either our prayers were not heard or, for some reason they were not answered in the ways we had asked them to be. And we are left to wonder why! Has God abandoned us? Does He not care about the circumstances of our lives? Has our faith in Him been in vain?

Folks, I want to remind you that we do not live in that nice, neat, comfortable, Christian society that we have all dreamed about. Actually, we live in a very pagan society that is not much different from the Babylonian empire in terms of its sinful influence and wicked behavior. And the fact is that it is very easy for us, as Christians, to forget about who we are, why we are here, and just blend in with the acceptable sins of our society.

In other words, it is easier for us to just go with the flow and be acceptable by the people than it is to remain true to the standards God has established for His people and suffer the persecution.

So, in the name of neighborliness we acquiesce to their way of life. We listen to their music or attend their places of entertainment. After all, there's nothing wrong with having a little fun, and quite frankly, we sort of envy the fellowship they are having with their friends. Then perhaps we compromise on a business deal to make a larger profit, because that is just the way it is done today. Or, we cheat on our income taxes or fudge on our expense account – everybody does it. We flirt with lust and immorality, even allowing it in out homes through television, magazines, movies and other kinds of media – after all, everybody's watching it today, and if we don't we won't be able to join the conversations at school or at work.

We begin to rationalize this sin or justify that sin, and before long there is no visible difference between the lifestyles of the believer and that of the unbeliever – not because the society has changed and pressured us into conformity, but because we allowed society to change us, rather than us changing society. Rather than allowing the increasing pressure from our sinful culture to cause us to turn more toward our Savior and away from the world, we have allowed our sinful culture to pressure us into conformity with its values. And in so doing, we have allowed the standard of our Lord fall into disgrace. And again, I say, **the saddest part of it all is that there is no great cry from God's people that that standard be raised again**.

I know the pressures upon Christians today are severe, and the battle to remain true to our calling is hard. But it is in the midst of the battle that the standard needs to be raised higher so that others who are struggling also can see it and have hope. When one of us falls, as we are all prone to do at some point and in some way, that should not cause the rest of us to follow that same path, or point fingers of judgment upon those who do. What it should do is to cause us to reach down in the pits of that sin and raise up that standard even higher, so that our fellow soldiers can see it and continue the march.

I'm sure we have all been affected by those believers who have fallen into sin – Presidents, pastors, parents, professionals and other personal friends; folks we believed in and trusted in and often confided in. And the destruction of their folly is far and wide. But, when a fellow soldier falls, rather than the rest of the "unit" wallowing in their disgrace, we must take heed, lest we too fall into an even greater sin. And rather than being defeated over it, we should raise up the standard in our own lives, even at the very point of their defeat.

For example, when a husband or wife cheats on their mates, or their marriage breaks down, we should raise the standard of our own marriage by being faithful to our own vows to our spouses, while we pray for those who have fallen. Or, when a friend lies, or steals or cheats, or they get involved in some immoral activity, we should raise the standards of our own walk with the Lord, and pray for those who have fallen.

If God seems far away today, I can assure you that He is

not the one who moved. He is still the same God He was when He moved your heart to accept His Son as your Savior, ever how many years ago that was. His love for you is still the same today as it was way back then; it's never changed and it never will. But it is your unconfessed sin that is keeping God at a distance from your heart. In Psalm 66:18, David said *"If I regard iniquity in my heart, the Lord will not hear me."*

There is one thing God cannot do – He cannot overlook sin! He can forgive it, cleanse it, even blot it out and forget it, if it is covered by the blood of Jesus Christ. If God is reminding you of that sin of compromise in your life right now, He is not doing that to condemn you, but to forgive you and to cleanse you of all unrighteousness. That feeling of guilt is not God's hand of judgment. It's God's way of telling you that He loves you and that He wants to free you from the condemnation of that sin, if you will only confess it – agree with Him that it is hindering your fellowship, your walk and your witness.

In Isaiah 59:12, the prophet Isaiah led the people in their prayer of confession and repentance: *"For our transgressions are multiplied before thee, and our sins testify against us; for our transgressions are with us; and as for our iniquities, we know them."*

- In verse 13 we see the sins of the heart and the tongue – *"In transgressing and lying against the Lord, and departing away from our God, speaking oppression and revolt, conceiving and uttering from the heart words of falsehood."*
- In verse 14 we see that, not only had they lied to each other, but they had also lied to the Lord – *"And judgment is turned away backward, and justice standeth afar off; for truth is fallen in the street, and equity cannot enter."*

Now, we must understand how difficult this time of confession and repentance was for the Hebrews. After all, they had rationalized and justified their sin for years. Or, they had excused it by blaming others, or even God for their behavior. But the day of reckoning had come. God was holding up the mirror of His Word and allowing His people to see the wickedness of their own heart and soul; it was time for true confessions.

Sometimes we are prone to carry the guilt of our sins for a long time, waiting for someone to come along and absolve us of our responsibility, or at least say they understand why we sinned the way we did. But when someone points out our sin, or we get caught in the act of sin, and we are forced to finally confess up, it's like we opened our heart and let go of all that built up frustration, guilt, bitterness, resentment, anger and hostility that we had been holding on to for years, and the release is wonderful.

But if we do not genuinely repent of that sin, the guilt will soon return, and the consequences will be even greater than before. Being sorry that we committed a sin is not genuine repentance, and neither is being sorry we got caught in sin, or that we hurt others by our sin. True repentance starts when we see how our sins have hurt the heart of God, and separated us from Him. Then, when we confess THAT sin, in addition to the sin(s) we have committed against Him, and we truly turn away from that sin and surrender our heart to Him, then, it can be said that we have genuinely repented. And the most glorious truth that we could ever know is that once God has forgiven us of our sins, He will cleanse us of all our unrighteousness (1 John 1:9) – it is "just-as-if-I'd-never-sinned"– and God will never, never, never, no never bring that sin to our memory again.

In Isaiah 59:16-21, the Bible tells us how God will one day restore His people to Himself; a pattern of how He wants to restore all sinners to Himself today. In verse 16,

Isaiah said, God *"saw that there was no man, and wondered that there was no intercessor."* God could not even find one man who stood for justice or cried out unto God in prayer for the people of Israel.

What a shame! The people of Israel – God's chosen people, stripped of their pride, their heritage, their blessings, even their very freedom; being held in bondage, and worked as slaves for a pagan people. Yet God could not find one man who was crying out unto God for His forgiveness, or one man who would dare to lead the people to cry out unto God. Where were their spiritual leaders? Where were those godly fathers and mothers who had been told how to raise their children and to pass down the heritage of their faith in God?

But rather than destroy His corrupted people, God put on the armor of war Himself, and prepared to do battle FOR HIS PEOPLE. The last part of verse 16 reads: *"Therefore His arm brought salvation unto Him (or for Him), and His own righteousness sustained Him."* And in verses 19-20 we read *"So shall they fear the name of the Lord from the west and his glory from the rising of the sun. When the enemy shall come in like a flood,* **the Spirit of the Lord shall lift up a standard against him.** *And the Redeemer shall come to Zion, and unto them that turn from transgression in Jacob, saith the Lord."* (Emphasis mine)

Isaiah is writing of that day, during the time of the Great Tribulation, when it appears the nation of Israel is doomed, and it is about to be destroyed. All of the armies of the world will be gathered there in the Valley of Megiddo to war against Israel over who is going to rule the world. There will not be one man on earth who can do anything to stop it – no peace treaty will be able to settle it; no peace accord can avoid it; no price can be paid to keep it from happening. When it appears that Israel is all but defeated, the sky is going to open up, and out of heaven's glory will ride the One who was called Faithful and True, whose name is called the Word of God. Riding behind Him are all the armies of heaven, and on Him is a name written: King of Kings and Lord of Lords.

Isaiah is speaking of that day when **God will raise up a standard against all the evil of the world, even since the day of Adam**. Isaiah is speaking of the second coming of Jesus Christ upon this earth, when He will, to paraphrase the song *"rule the world with truth and grace, and make the nations prove, the glories of His righteousness, and the wonders of His love. No more will sin and sorrow reign, nor will thorns infest the ground. He will remove the plague of sin, far as that curse is found."*

We may think we are in such a terrible condition today that there is no way out, and the enemy is upon us just like a flood. But our way out is up, and all we need to do is to turn to Jesus, and He will raise that standard within us; that is the indwelling presence of the Holy Spirit, who will guide us, protect us, keep us and perfect us until Jesus comes and takes us home to be with Him forever. And from my point of view, that day is very soon!

Epilogue

My y purpose in writing this book **was to urge every true, born-again believer to stand up for Jesus, as soldiers of the cross; to lift high His royal banner, for God knows it has suffered enough loss.** I urge every Christian to join hearts and arms with every other Christian in their home, their family, their community; their church, and begin the march, from victory unto victory, with Jesus in the lead; till every foe is vanquished, till that day when Jesus Christ is Lord indeed!

It is time we put away all the songs, the books, and the nice little stories about God, and the trite little clichés and the irreverent logos, that often profane the very Name and the very nature of God, and get back to the real word of God as our only source of truth, and therefore our guide for our daily lives. We must measure our lives by the standard set forth in God's word, and not rationalize and justify our sins any longer. A lost and dying world is waiting to see what God can do with one man who is totally devoted to Him. **Are you willing to raise the standard in your own walk with the Lord, even if no one else does, or even cares that you do? Are you willing to suffer the persecution if you do? But more importantly, are you ready to answer to the Lord if you don't?**

What will it take to get our attention? How many more earthquakes, floods, tsunamis or other so called "natural disasters" must God allow, or even engineer to get our attention? How many more physical, emotional or mental diseases must we face, for which we can find no cure, until we realize we cannot dishonor God without incurring the reasonable consequences for our sins? How many more families must be destroyed, or children be abandoned, or teenagers allowed to ruin their lives, until we finally repent of our sin, and return to God's Word and God's ways regarding the family? How many more churches must be divided and their witness to the world discredited before we realize that the Church belongs to the Lord; it really is His Body, and He has given us the responsibility to keep it pure until He calls it to Himself.

Must God lift His hand of protection from our nation another time to remind us of how He has blessed us? Will we have to lose our freedom before we realize what we had? Must we be forced to forfeit our Christian heritage and traditions before we long to truly worship God again?

I ask every husband and father to raise the standard of Jesus Christ in his own family, beginning with his own personal walk with the Lord, and then allowing that change to affect the rest of his family. **I ask every wife and mother** not only to agree to that decision, but to support it, enhance it, and to do whatever she can to see that it happens. This will take time, and you can expect some severe opposition from those who are enjoying their freedom and lack of conviction. You might also incur some testing of your commitment along the way, even some ridicule from those you thought would be very supportive. Just remember, making that decision to allow Jesus Christ to be the Lord of your life is the most difficult part. But if you will take that step of faith, God Himself will guide you into each subsequent step, for His name sake.

I ask every true, God-called Pastor/Preacher to

review his calling to make sure it is from the Lord, and to honor that calling with a new commitment to raise the standard of excellence in his preaching. The Apostle Paul said, as preachers, we are *"stewards of the mysteries of God...moreover it is required in stewards, that a man be found faithful."* (Ephesians 4:1-2) Notice it did not say successful or profitable or even well loved by his congregations. But he is to be faithful in teaching and preaching the word of God, just as it is written; just as it has been given to him, and leaving the results to the Holy Spirit.

In that marvelous, insightful book, *The Reformed Pastor,* the puritan Pastor Richard Baxter wrote:

> *"take heed to yourselves, that you want {lack} not the qualifications necessary for your work. He must not be himself a babe in knowledge, that will teach men all those mysterious things which must be known in order to salvation....this is not a burden for the shoulders of a child...so great a God, whose message we deliver, should be honored by our delivery of it. It is a lamentable case, that in a message from the God of heaven, of everlasting moment to the souls of men, we should behave ourselves so weakly, so unhandsomely, so imprudently, or so slightly, that the whole business should miscarry in our hands, and God should be dishonored, and his work disgraced, and sinners rather hardened than converted; and all this through our weakness or neglect."* (*The Reformed Pastor*, The Banner Of Truth Trust, Reprinted, 2001)

The Apostle Paul exhorted **every believer to:**

"Study to show thyself approved unto God; a workman that needeth not to be ashamed, rightly dividing

the word of truth; Shun profane and vain babblings; for they will increase unto more ungodliness." (2 Timothy 3:15-16)

If that is the duty and responsibility of every true believer, then how much more should it apply to those who are privileged to teach and preach God's Word.

Many young men are being called to pastor churches today without a solid background in Biblical knowledge, or without any tools to help them learn to preach effectively. While it would be good if they could obtain such training in a formal setting, so as to interact and fellowship with those who are also studying the same subjects and wrestling with the same issues, the real meat of the training is available now in correspondence form, off-campus classes, week-long sessions, or via the internet.

The tragedy is that many will only preach what they hear others preach and try to "make" the message theirs; it's the Saturday night cop-out! But their people will know the difference; so will the preacher, and so will the One who sent him to preach, and who gave him the message. Someone said, "A message designed in your mind will reach a mind. A message designed in your heart will reach a heart. But a message that is designed in your life will change a life." In Philippians 4:9, the Apostle Paul said *"The things you have learned and received and heard and seen in me, practice these things, and the God of peace will be with you."* (NASB) **If we really want our sermons to change lives, we must be living examples of every truth we dare to preach!**

In Jeremiah 33:12-13, the prophet wrote of that day which is to come, when God will raise up *"a habitation of shepherds who will rest their flocks...the flocks shall again pass under the hands of the one who numbers them, says the Lord."* Rather than counting the numbers on Sunday, perhaps it would be more beneficial for a pastor to let every church member know they count; that they are important to the family of God. **Many of today's younger pastors don't want to visit their sick members, or even get involved in the hurts and heartaches of their lives. But God did not call us just to preach to the masses; He called us to get involved in their messes,** and to show them how Jesus Christ can make a difference in their lives. There is no way that can be done in a congregational sermon on Sunday. That must be done in their homes, by their bedside, at the moment of crisis, at the time of need. That is where we earn the right to be heard every Sunday!

In a day when all kinds of market research can tell us just about everything we want to know about our society and our culture, **perhaps it would be better if we were less concerned about what "the latest survey shows" and more concerned about "thus saith the Lord!"** Preachers are not to compare the behavior of God's people to the standards of the world, but to the standards of the Word of God. We must raise that standard in our own eyes if we are to raise it in theirs, and that includes our belief in and our trust in the divinely inspired, infallible and inerrant Word of God as our only source of truth regarding our faith and the way we practice it.

I am calling upon every minister of music to raise the standard of worship music. The easiest thing to do is to join one of the camps and dig in for the battle. The hardest thing to do is to search God's word for what He has said about music; its place in our worship and the problems in can cause. In planning worship music, I believe we must keep one foot firmly planted in the great songs of faith, those that teach doctrinal truths as well as express the very character of God, Christ and the Holy Spirit. But I also believe we must allow the other foot to continually search all the songs and all the music that has been written, and is being written today, examine it in the light of Holy Scripture, and incorporate that which meets our standard into the worship service. **Our concern should not be whether it is traditional or contemporary, but does it lead us to worship God.**

Our concern should not be whether it attracts people or pleases people, but whether or not it is acceptable worship unto God. Pastors and worship leaders must work together to achieve a harmonious relationship, especially during the worship services, or else we will continue to divide our people over this issue, and fail to lead them into genuine, God-focused worship.

Finally I encourage the faithful remnant to not give up, give out or give in just yet, for your prayers are about to be answered. Even the publication of this book is an indication that some things in the church are about to change. I give you two admonitions, one from scripture and the other by way of testimony.

The first admonition is found in James 1:19-20: *"This you know, my beloved. But let everyone be quick to hear, slow to speak and slow to anger; for the anger of man does not achieve the righteousness of God."* (NASB) If your Pastor or music leader has adopted a style of worship and music that is not supportive of your personal spiritual growth, or conducive to your worship, talk to them about it, but do your homework first; otherwise it will simply be your opinion and tastes versus theirs, and there will be no healing of the breech. The bibliography at the end of this book will list several authors that deal with this issue even more scripturally than I have attempted to do here. I urge you to read those books, study the passages of God's Word that they have referred to, and pray for God's wisdom and God's will to be done. Then, make an appointment with your Pastor and/or worship leaders; ask them to allow you to share your heart, in love, and then let God rule in their hearts. Above all be *"diligent to preserve the unity of the Spirit in the bond of* *peace."* (Ephesians 4:3 NASB)

The second admonition comes from the late Dr. Herschel Hobbs. I was writing a paper in Bible college on the Baptists and the Bible; the battle over inerrancy. Since Dr. Hobbs had written most of the doctrinal commentary in his book, *What Baptists Believe*, I wrote him a letter, asking him to clarify some statements he made regarding the Bible, and closed the letter by telling him I did not have an "axe to grind, but one to sharpen!"

Several weeks later I received a hand-written letter from Dr. Hobbs; one I will cherish for the rest of my life. After explaining his position on the issues, Dr. Hobbs closed his letter with this personal challenge. *"My dear young preacher boy, I urge you to remain faithful to the Word of God. Others may chase theological rabbits, but one day, they will come and sit at your feet!"* As you can see, now 30 years later, I have never forgotten that challenge, or the inspiration it gave me to never compromise my convictions.

I have many friends in many different churches who are struggling to stay committed to their church for one reason or the other. My challenge to them is to **remain faithful in their calling at that church, and true to the teachings of the Word of God** in whatever position they hold. Sooner or later the bad of this fad will fade and the good will remain, just as it has always been. And those who have wandered away in search of more exciting pastors, or styles of worship, or more relevant Bible study, or something different for their particular age group, will return and sit at your feet. *"For all flesh is like grass, and all its glory is like the flower of grass. The grass withers, and the flower falls off, but the Word of the Lord abides forever."* (1 Peter 1:24-25 NASB) Amen and Amen!

For the apparent good the contemporary movement has had on making the church more relevant to the people, it has had an equal, if not greater detriment by

lowering the people's concept of God. We are at a point right now in our culture where the absolute authority of God's Word, the awesome majesty of God's power, the amazing sufficiency of God's grace, and the astounding influence of His love could have a greater impact than at any other time in the history of the world. We cannot do that by lowering the standards of God's character to make Him more relevant to man. We can only do that by lifting up the Standard of the Lord, Jesus Christ, and He will draw lost man to God.

General Douglas MacArthur saw our withdrawal from the Philippines as a stain upon America's honor. He said, *"Until we lift our flag from the dust, we are a disgrace to the rest of the world!"* Dear believer, until we lift the Standard of Jesus Christ up from the dust of compromise, complacency and convenience, everything else we do to make our churches more successful will be like a band-aid on a gushing wound.

Thirty-one years ago I was inducted into the army of the Lord. I became a soldier, under the command of the Lord Jesus Christ. For hundreds of years, thousands of fellow soldiers lived, fought and often died in their fight to lift high His royal banner. Now, the standard has been handed to me and to the others in my generation. If I should die before the rapture of the church, I pray that my body will be found close to the standard of the Lord Jesus Christ, with my hands stretched out, trying to lift it up!

"Unto Him be glory in the church
by Christ Jesus
throughout all ages,
world without end!"

(Ephesians 3:21)

ADDENDUM ONE

A Statement Added to the Baptist Faith and Message Regarding the Sanctity of Marriage and the Family

"God has ordained the family as the foundational institution of human society. It is composed of persons related to one another by marriage, blood or adoption. Marriage is the uniting of one man and one woman in covenant commitment for a lifetime. It is God's unique gift to provide for the man and the woman in marriage the framework for intimate companionship, the channel for sexual expression according to Biblical standards, and the means for the procreation of the human race. The husband and wife are of equal worth before God. Both bear God's image, but in differing ways. The marriage relationship models the way God relates to His people. A husband is to love his wife as Christ loved the Church, and he has the God given responsibility to provide for, to protect and to lead his family. A wife is to submit graciously to the servant leadership of her husband, even as the church willingly submits to the headship of Christ. She, being in the image of God, as is her husband thus equal to him, has the God given responsibility to respect her husband, and to serve as his helper in managing their household and nurturing the next generation."

Approved by the messengers at the Southern Baptist Convention, June 1998

Selected Bibliography

Richard Baxter, *The Reformed Pastor,* (The Banner of Truth Trust, reprinted 2001)

William J. Bennett, *The Death of Outrage: Bill Clinton and the Assault on American Ideals* (Free Press, 1998)

Robert H. Bork, *Slouching Towards Gomorrah: Modern Liberalism and American Decline* (HarperCollins Publishers, 1996)

Oswald Chambers, *My Utmost for His Highest* (Dodd, Mead & Company, 1935)

Charles Colson and Nancy Pearcey, *How Shall We Live?* (Tyndale House Publishers, Inc.)

Marva J. Dawn, *Reaching Out Without Dumbing Down: A Theology of Worship for This Urgent Time* (William B. Eerdmans Publishing Company, 1995)

Philip Graham Ryken, Derek W.H. Thomas, J. Ligon Duncan III, editors, *Give Praise to God; A Vision for Reforming Worship, celebrating the legacy of James Montgomery Boice* (R&R Publishing, 2003)

Os Guinness, *Time for Truth: Living Free in a world of Lies, Hype, & Spin,* (Baker Books, 2000)

Michael Horton, *A Better Way: Rediscovering the Drama of God-centered Worship* (Baker Books, 2002)

John MacArthur, *Truth Matters: Landmark Chapters from the Teaching Ministry of John MacArthur* (Thomas Nelson Publishers, 2004)

John Piper, *Desiring God: Meditations of a Christian Hedonist* (Multnomah Publishers, 2003)

John Phillips, Exploring The Psalms, Volumes One and Two (Loizeaux Brothers, 1988)

Derek Prime & Alistair Begg, *On Being A Pastor: Understanding Our Calling and Our Work* (Moody Publishers, 2004)

Fred L. Volz, *Strange Fire: Confessions of a False Prophet* (Trion Press Publishing, 2003)

With Sincere Appreciation

To my former Pastors, Rev. Donald P. Davis, Dr. C. Robert Marsh, Dr. Nelson Price, Dr. Charles Q. Carter, and my dear Pastor friend, Dr. Paul VanGorder, who, in their own unique way, helped to establish the standard of excellence in my mind of what it means to be a true man of God – a preacher and a pastor.

To my former Ministers of Music, Rev. John Condra, Rev. Irvin Perry, and to my co-laborer in the Lord, Rev. Paul Robins, who helped to establish the standard of excellence in my mind of what it means to truly worship God through music.

To Dr. Stephen F. Olford, and his son Dr. David Olford, who, through the Institute For Biblical Preaching, helped to establish in the standard of excellence in my mind regarding true, expository preaching. Without a doubt, this was the most transforming three weeks of my entire ministry.

To my son, Rev. Steven B. Edwards, and his gracious wife, Vanessa, who are setting the standard of excellence of what it means to be a godly husband and father, wife and mother, before our precious granddaughter, Elizabeth.

To my dear wife, Linda, who has set the standard of excellence in what it means to be a virtuous woman, a faithful wife, a godly mother, a loving grandmother, and the highest example of what it means to serve the Lord as a Pastor's wife.

To Caroline Ward and Debra Neyland, friends and former disciples who set the standard of excellence for this book and graciously gave their editorial assistance to achieve it.

MATURE MINISTRIES

"...Until we all obtain to the unity of the faith, and of the knowledge of the Son of God, to a mature man, to the measure of the stature which belongs to the fullness of Christ." Ephesians 4:13

**A REVIVAL MINISTRY, ENCOURAGING GOD'S PEOPLE TO RAISE THE STANDARD OF RIGHTEOUSNESS IN THEIR LIVES
WAYNE J. EDWARDS, FOUNDER AND SPEAKER.**

Revival Topics Available

Raising The Standard - Lifting up the Lord Jesus Christ in our worship, our walk and our witness.

Your Family: Beating the Odds - How to have a godly marriage and raise godly children in an ungodly society.

I love My Church - What it means to be the Body of Christ in the world today.

Spiritual Leadership - The essential qualities of those God uses to accomplish His work in His way, and for His glory.

Bring Back The Glory - Restoring Biblical integrity and spiritual power to the church.

The Victorious Christian Life - Living a life that is wholly devoted to Jesus. (A study of Romans 7-8)

The Age Of The Apocalypse - Living in the last days of the church age. (A study of the book of Revelation)

Heartcry for Revival – Removing the "fleshly" things that hinder our personal intimacy with God.

Other topics available upon request.

FOR INFORMATION OR FOR BOOKING A CONFERENCE CONTACT:

**Mature Ministries, Inc.
PO Box 87,
Martin, Ga. 30557
(706) 779-5158**
E-mail wnledwards@alltel.net

CPSIA information can be obtained at www.ICGtesting.com
Printed in the USA
LVOW11s0708190114

369934LV00001B/2/P

9 781597 814720